Formula 1 99

The Grand Prix Season

Jean-Michel Desnoues
Patrick Camus
Jean-Marc Loubat / Vandystadt

Queen Anne Press
is a division of Lennard Associates Ltd
Mackerye End, Harpenden, Herts AL5 5DR

© 1999 Source Publishing Genève CH Suisse
English language edition © Lennard Associates Ltd

ISBN 1 85291 606 0

British Library Cataloguing in Publication data is available

Editorial consultant: Simon Arron
Page design: Dominique Gambier
Editor for Queen Anne Press: Chris Marshall

Printed and bound in Great Britain by
Butler & Tanner Ltd, Frome and London

Formula 1 99

The Grand Prix Season

Teams / Drivers / Circuits / Statistics

Jean-Michel Desnoues
Patrick Camus
Jean-Marc Loubat / Vandystadt

Queen Anne Press

Foreword

Welcome to *Formula 1 99*. After realising my lifetime ambition by clinching the world championship title at Suzuka last year, I have received no shortage of congratulations and good advice – not to mention warnings about what my status as world champion involved. Nobody cautioned me, however, that I would have to fulfil a few journalistic roles. Perhaps I could think of this as warming up for a new career once I retire. Still, as I don't have any fixed plans on that subject – and I haven't yet reached my sell-by date – I can assure the writing profession (in particular Patrick Camus and Jean-Michel Desnoues) that there will be no competition between us...this year, at least.

In fact, I have told myself that winning a first world title is the best possible preparation for winning a second. And that's the clear goal I have set myself this season. I want to win as many races as possible on the tracks about which you will be learning a great deal on the following pages. And I want to keep ahead of all other drivers – especially the bloke in red overalls driving car number three! By the time we get back to Japan, I would like to have my second championship in the bag. I haven't yet checked to see whether *Formula 1 99* is hoping for the same outcome...

On a more serious note, I am not under any illusions. It's going to be a tough campaign. Last year we had to cope with a number of new regulations and the West McLaren Mercedes team adapted better than the rest. Inevitably, however, things have moved on. The opposition has taken on board the lessons of last season, drawn a few conclusions and certainly learned from some of what we did to strengthen their own hand in areas where they were previously weak. That's why McLaren's powers-that-be took on a bold challenge and decided to stretch the boundaries of technology even further. No question, the new McLaren MP4-14 is very quick, but I'm expecting stiff opposition from Ferrari and I'm sure that my team-mate David Coulthard is going to be an even tougher rival than before, in every sense of the word. But other teams have made good progress, too. And that makes me think results this season could be just as surprising as the races are fascinating.

For you, the spectator, 1999 promises to be a good vintage. Not just because a greater number of teams and drivers will have the chance to joust for victory, or at least podium finishes, but also because F1 has gone back to having a single tyre supplier in Bridgestone. That means the input of the driver will be more important – absolutely vital, in fact. And there's another thing that gives 1999 an extra spark. To begin with, the addition of a fourth groove to the front tyres was designed to slow cars down, but we have quickly seen how the ingenuity of the designers, engine builders and aerodynamicists has kept performance at 1998 levels – and we will doubtless be better at some tracks. But I'd prefer it if I were the only one to set new standards.

I hope you will derive as much pleasure from watching as I will from driving and hope to see you here again for another foreword in 12 months – at the most.

Mika Hakkinen

The Flying Finn
World Champion

1999 Calendar

Contents

Entry list 1999

1. M. Hakkinen (Finland)
McLaren-Mercedes MP4-14 Bridgestone
2. D. Coulthard (Great Britain)
McLaren-Mercedes MP4-14 Bridgestone
3. M. Schumacher (Germany)
Ferrari-Ferrari F399 Bridgestone
4. E. Irvine (Great Britain)
Ferrari-Ferrari F399 Bridgestone
5. A. Zanardi (Italy)
Williams-Supertec FW21 Bridgestone
6. Ralf Schumacher (Germany)
Williams-Supertec FW21 Bridgestone
7. D. Hill (Great Britain)
Jordan-Mugen-Honda 199 Bridgestone
8. H.H. Frentzen (Germany)
Jordan-Mugen-Honda 199 Bridgestone
9. G. Fisichella (Italy)
Benetton-Supertec B199 Bridgestone
10. A. Wurz (Austria)
Benetton-Supertec B199 Bridgestone
11. J. Alesi (France)
Sauber-Pétronas C18 Bridgestone
12. P. Diniz (Brazil)
Sauber-Pétronas C18 Bridgestone
14. T. Takagi (Japan)
Arrows-Arrows A20 Bridgestone
15. P. de la Rosa (Italy)
Arrows-Arrows A20 Bridgestone
16. R. Barrichello (Brazil)
Stewart-Ford SF-3 Bridgestone
17. J. Herbert (Great Britain)
Stewart-Ford SF-3 Bridgestone
18. O. Panis (France)
Prost-Peugeot AP02 Bridgestone
19. J. Trulli (Italy)
Prost-Peugeot AP02 Bridgestone
20. M. Gené (Spain)
Minardi-Ford Zetec-R M01 Bridgestone
21. L. Badoer (Italy)
Minardi-Ford Zetec-R M01 Bridgestone
22. J. Villeneuve (Canada)
BAR-Supertec PR01 Bridgestone
23. R. Zonta (Brazil)
BAR-Supertec PR01 Bridgestone

Teams
and Drivers

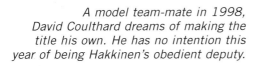

Will last year's united front between Hakkinen and Coulthard survive the British driver's pledge to chase the title?

A model team-mate in 1998, David Coulthard dreams of making the title his own. He has no intention this year of being Hakkinen's obedient deputy.

**Mercedes FO110H
(built by Ilmor)
72-degree V10
Capacity: 2998cc
Power: 800bhp plus
Weight: 105kg**

Address:	McLaren International Ltd, Unit 22, Woking Business Park, Albert Drive, Woking, Surrey GU21 5JY, England
Tel:	(44) 0148 372 8211
Fax:	(44) 0148 372 0157
Internet:	www.mclaren.co.uk
Number of staff:	350
First GP:	Monaco 1966
GP starts:	476
Wins:	116
First win:	Belgium 1968 (Bruce McLaren)
Poles:	92
Fastest laps:	80
Points scored:	2205.5 (average per GP: 4.63)
World constructors' titles:	8 (74, 84, 85, 88, 89, 90, 91, 98)
World drivers' titles:	10 (Fittipaldi 74; Hunt 76; Lauda 84; Prost 85, 86, 89; Senna 88, 90, 91; Hakkinen 98)
Test driver:	Nick Heidfeld (Germany)
1998 record:	World champion (156pts)

Chairman:
Ron Dennis

Technical director:
Adrian Newey

• Plus points
On the crest of a wave
First-class technical resources
Financial muscle
Strong driver line-up

• Minus points
Competition between drivers
Emphasis on speed rather than reliability?
No longer has any tyre advantage

MERCEDES
McLaren

McLaren MP4-14 – Tyres Bridgestone

The MP4-14 looks even more effective than its predecessor, but will it be as reliable? Mika Hakkinen certainly hopes so – he's keen to hang on to his title.

Ron Dennis does not want to return to the difficult days of the mid-Nineties at any price – and that's why he has not allowed his men to slack one inch during the winter break. Now that he is back at the summit, the Woking team chief wants to end the "Williams" era for once and for all and to stamp his own identity on the third millennium's first decade. To realise his ambitions, Dennis wasn't happy merely to touch up the title-winning MP4-13 – a car that still had plenty to offer. Instead, Adrian Newey, Neil Oatley and aerodynamicist Henri Durand started with a clean sheet of paper. Why not strike even more fear into rivals who, on the surface, seem to be steering a more conservative course? That said, technical bravery has built-in risks, as the first race in Melbourne showed only too clearly. So, are the Silver Arrows still invincible?

Fortified by his first world title win last year, Mika Hakkinen has silenced his critics and now has his eyes firmly on a double.

Although its reliability has yet to be established, the McLaren MP4-14 is already something of a benchmark. And it looks even more capable of taking Hakkinen to the crown than last year's machine.

Date and place of birth:	28 September 1968, Helsinki, Finland
Nationality:	Finnish
Lives in:	Monte Carlo
Marital status:	married to Erja
Height/Weight:	1.79m/70kg
Hobbies :	water sports, squash, tennis, cross-country skiing, pop music
Favourite food and drink:	Finnish cuisine, apple juice and fizzy water
First race:	USA 1991 (Lotus)
F1 statistics:	Reigning world champion. 113 starts, 218 points, 9 wins, 11 pole positions
F1 record:	**1991**: Lotus-Judd. 15th in the championship with 2pts. **1992**: Lotus-Ford. 11th, 11pts. **1993**: McLaren-Ford. Took part in 3 grands prix. 3rd in the Japanese GP. 15th, 4pts. **1994**: McLaren-Peugeot. 2nd in the Belgian GP, 3rd in San Marino, Silverstone, Monza, Estoril and Jerez. 4th, 26pts. **1995**: McLaren-Mercedes. 2nd in Italy and Japan. 7th, 17pts. **1996**: McLaren-Mercedes. 3rd at Silverstone, Spa, Monza and Suzuka. 5th, 31pts. **1997**: McLaren-Mercedes. 3 podiums. First win at Jerez. 6th, 27pts. **1998**: McLaren-Mercedes. 8 wins, 2nd at Buenos Aires and Silverstone. 11 podiums. World champion, 100pts. **1999**: McLaren-Mercedes.

Number 1

McLaren - Mercedes

Mika Hakkinen

There's not much that hasn't been written about Hakkinen. It was said his terrible accident in Adelaide in 1995 would finish his career, or at least stifle his hunger for victory. Some thought self-doubt would lead him to crumble, psychologically, against the robust Schumacher. Others thought his team-mate Coulthard would be too fast to let him achieve his ultimate goal, or that the strict approach of Ron Dennis and Mercedes wouldn't give him the option of showing his true colours. Every pundit was wrong.

Hakkinen has put the accident behind him. He refuses to discuss it, or even to look at pictures. As for Schumacher, the Finn made up for a couple of missed opportunities and went on to resist everything the German could throw at him, even in the toughest situations. The stress level peaked in the 1998 Japanese GP, just as Schumacher appeared to be blocking Hakkinen's route to the title. Ferrari president Luca di Montezemolo could have claimed Hakkinen had a car that any one of several drivers could have taken to the title – just as he did when Villeneuve triumphed for Williams-Renault in 1997. But is that necessarily the case? Is having the best car a good thing or a bad thing?

"It can be a big handicap," recalls Alain Prost, "because it automatically makes you favourite. Your are obliged to take pole position, win the race, set the fastest lap and take the championship. Morally it's torture because as soon as you slip up even slightly you are suddenly regarded as the worst driver of all time."

Hakkinen avoided all these potential pitfalls. And there's no reason to suppose he won't be just as strong this season. His car might prove not to be reliable enough, but he is ready.

Pole position winner in Melbourne, he is hot favourite to win again.

17

Dominated by team-mate Hakkinen last year and forced by mid-season to play a back-up role to the Finn, David Coulthard is keen for revenge. But if he wants to fight for the title, the Scot needs to show from the off that he is a match for the world champion.

Although Coulthard doesn't have the same relationship with the Woking team as the longer-serving Hakkinen, he has nonetheless gained their acceptance and respect. And if he shows himself capable of beating Hakkinen, Ron Dennis will give him carte blanche to do so.

Date and place of birth:	27 March 1971, Twynholm, Scotland
Nationality:	British
Lives in:	Monte Carlo
Marital status:	single, lives with Heidi
Height/Weight:	1.82m/74kg
Hobbies:	golf, cycling, tennis, swimming, and music
Favourite food:	Italian cuisine
First race:	Spain 1994 (Williams)
F1 statistics:	3rd in 1995 (Williams), 1997 and 1998 (McLaren). 75 starts, 173 points, 3 wins, 5 pole positions
F1 record:	**1994**: Williams-Renault test driver, called to replace late Ayrton Senna. GP debut in Spain. 8th in the championship with 14pts. **1995**: Williams-Renault. 1st win in Portugal. 7 podiums, 5 pole positions. 3rd, 49pts. **1996**: McLaren-Mercedes. 2nd in Monaco and 3rd at the Nürburgring. 7th, 18pts. **1997**: McLaren-Mercedes. Won in Australia and Italy, 2nd in Austria and at the Nürburgring. 4 podiums. 3rd, 36pts. **1998**: McLaren-Mercedes. Winner in San Marino, 2nd in Australia, Brazil, Spain, Austria, Germany and Hungary. 9 podiums, 3rd, 56pts. **1999**: McLaren-Mercedes.

Number 2

McLaren - Mercedes

David Coulthard

In his sixth season of F1, Coulthard desperately wants to succeed Damon Hill as the next British world champion.

Despite his first-class attitude, ideal upbringing and Hollywood smile, David Coulthard is under a cloud at the moment. After getting the better of Damon Hill at Williams, he joined McLaren in the hope of establishing himself as a team leader. And it looked a distinct possibility when he gave his new colleagues their first Mercedes-powered victory at Melbourne in 1997.

Unfortunately, however, he has not been able to maintain that bright form. People still wonder the extent to which Ron Dennis imposed team orders in the first race of 1998, when Coulthard waved Hakkinen through. If such politics exist, however, McLaren is a lot subtler about it than Ferrari. As the year wore on, Coulthard increasingly found he was drawn into what he felt was the ill-fitting role of deputy. Ironically, however, that could spur him on to good effect this time.

What qualities of leadership are lacking? A bit of self-confidence, perhaps? A touch of luck? It would help if he could be quick on a more consistent basis and work harder sorting out his car. Mika Hakkinen currently has the edge. And not only will it be tough for Coulthard to drag himself out of the Finn's shadow, but if he does it could unsettle their strong working relationship. Not that the Scot has

any choice. Another season like the last would establish him as a professional number two in the Irvine mould, and that would hasten his departure from McLaren because Ron Dennis wants two winners. And if he got a place with another team, it wouldn't be one that offered the same level of opportunity as McLaren. Hence 1999 is a vital season in terms of his racing future.

The Scuderia is mocked by a 20-year spell without a world drivers' title, as a successor to Jody Scheckter has still to be found. For Jean Todt's troops, the moment has come to wipe that slate clean.

Go! A new campaign is under way – and it's riddled with potential pitfalls for the Scuderia. After 20 seasons of repeated failure, it is time to take the title back to Maranello.

Ferrari 048
80-degree V10
Capacity: 2997cc
Dimensions not disclosed
Weight not disclosed

Address:	Ferrari Spa, Via Ascari 55/57, 41053 Maranello, Modena, Italy
Tel:	00 39 0536 94 11 61
Fax:	00 39 0536 94 64 88
Internet:	www.ferrari.it
First GP:	Monaco 1950
GP starts:	603
Wins:	119
First win:	Britain 1951 (Froilan Gonzales)
Poles:	124
Fastest laps:	133
Points scored:	2226.5 (average per GP: 3.69)
World constructors' titles:	8 (61, 64, 75, 76, 77, 79, 82, 83)
World drivers' titles:	9 (Ascari 52, 53; Fangio 56; Hawthorn 58; P. Hill 61; Surtees 64; Lauda 75, 77; Scheckter 79)
Test driver:	Luca Badoer (Italy)
1998 record:	2nd (133pts)

Sporting director:
Jean Todt

Technical director:
Ross Brawn

• **Plus points**
Stability of the engineering department
The influence of Michael Schumacher
Use of dependable technology
No more doubts about tyre parity

• **Minus points**
Have they been too conservative?
Is Fiat prepared to invest to the same degree as Mercedes?

Ferrari

Ferrari F399 – Tyres Bridgestone

Surprise winner of the opening grand prix in Melbourne, Eddie Irvine began his season with new ambitions. But will he be permitted to fulfil them later in the year?

There was no fanfare when Ferrari president Luca di Montezemolo announced his team's objective for the season ahead. The task, he said, was simply to do better than they had in 1998. From Jean Todt to Ross Brawn, from Rory Byrne to Paolo Martinelli, the message was received and understood by everybody. Nevertheless, even though the team benefits from a degree of continuity, the F399 chassis represents a fresh start for Ferrari.

Although it is described as an evolution of last year's car, the revisions have been fundamental and absolute – so much so that not a single component of the 1998 car has been carried over. And the latest V10 has been subjected to just as thorough a reworking. The revised engine installation has yielded a lower centre of gravity, which will benefit the chassis, and weight has also been pared (the new car is 6kg lighter). It remains to be seen whether all this will be enough ...

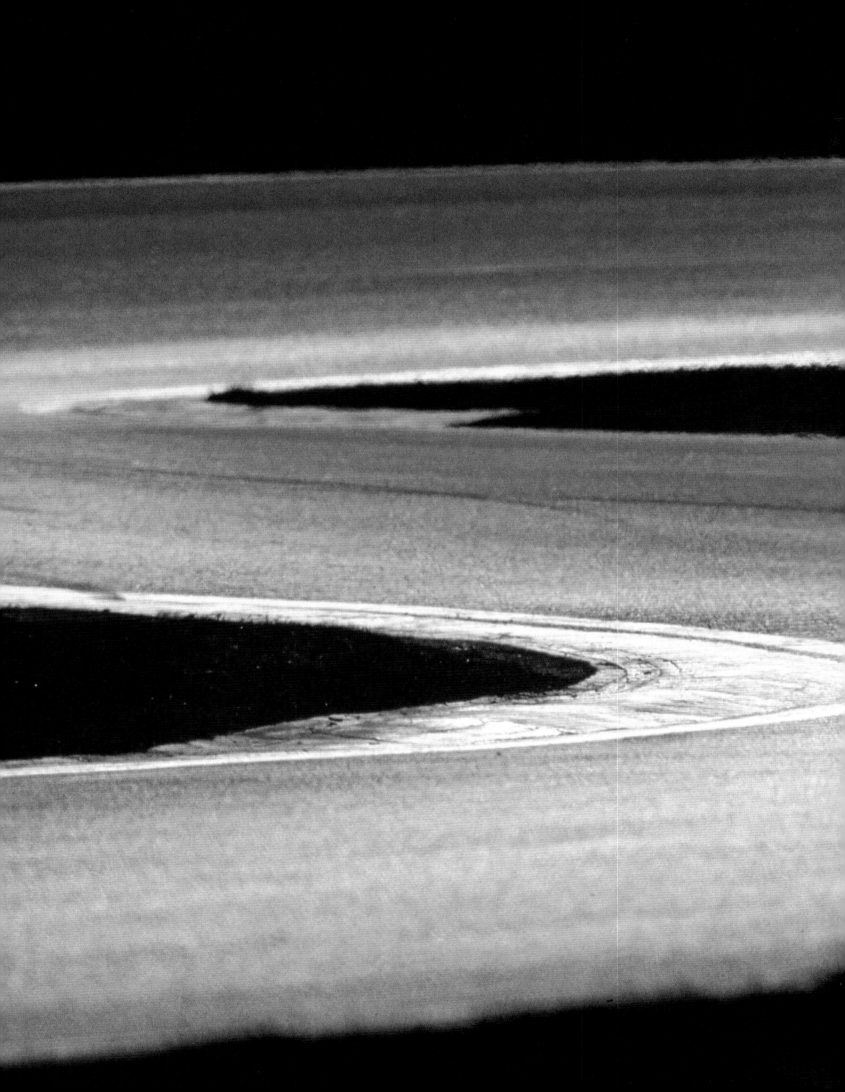

In contention for the title until the final race for two years running, Michael Schumacher does not want to see the crown escape him in that way again. And if that is to happen the Scuderia has to be competitive from race one.

What is the true potential of the F399? The chances of seeing a Schuey victory wave hinge on the answer. Irvine's victory in Australia notwithstanding, the early evidence was barely convincing – but you shouldn't underestimate the team's capacity to react to problems.

Date and place of birth:	3 January 1969, Hürth-Hermühlheim, Germany
Nationality:	German
Lives in:	Villers sur Ollon, Switzerland
Marital status:	married to Corinna, daughter Gina Maria and son Mick
Height/Weight:	1.74m/74kg
Hobbies:	karting, football, mountain biking, diving, going to the cinema and watch collecting
Favourite food and drink:	Italian cuisine, apple juice with fizzy water
First race:	Belgium 1991 (Jordan)
F1 statistics:	World champion in 1994 and 1995 (Benetton). 119 starts, 526 points, 33 wins, 20 pole positions
F1 record:	**1991**: Seventh on the grid for his first race in Belgium (Jordan). Fifth in Italy, his second race (Benetton). 12th in the championship with 4pts. **1992**: Benetton-Ford. 1st win in Portugal. 3rd, 53pts. **1993**: Benetton-Ford. Won in Portugal. 4th, 52pts. **1994**: Benetton-Ford. 8 wins. World champion, 92pts. **1995**: Benetton-Renault. 9 wins. World champion, 102pts. **1996**: Ferrari. 3 wins. 3rd, 59pts. **1997**: Ferrari. 5 wins. 2nd in championship but excluded from the results following his accident with Villeneuve at Jerez. **1998**: Ferrari. 6 wins. 2nd, 86pts. **1999**: Ferrari.

Number 3

Ferrari Michael Schumacher

So what was Schumacher looking for when he signed a three-year deal with Ferrari at the end of 1995? If he wanted to add to the consecutive world titles he had won with Benetton, it was a bum move. As a result, he has now extended his deal with the team until 2002. But even then there's no guarantee he will succeed. The seasons roll by and the man regarded as the best driver in the world finds he is standing still. Whose fault is that? It's not down to him, because he's the best in the business. That said, however...

In 1997 he ended his chances by ramming Villeneuve. In 1998 he opened the door for Hakkinen by stalling on the grid at Suzuka. The same happened again in the first race of this season in Australia, so is he victim or culprit? According to some within the team, he's to blame. But no one is apparently brave enough to tell him as much. In truth, however, he has proved himself to be the best driver in the world and all the evidence suggests his equipment is not up to the job. Last year the car suffered while it was being made to work well on its Goodyear tyres; this time there are signs that it needs a while to adapt to Bridgestone.

Life is seldom straightforward. It's a shame for Schumacher, because he has what it takes to match Fangio's record of five titles. And he could perhaps have beaten it but for the past three years of frustration with Ferrari. He has the talent, the support of watchdog Irvine, a team entirely at his service and the grudging admiration of his rivals, who know to get out of his way when the Ferrari is on song. But one day, when it's time to look back at this period in the sport's history, what will be written if this combination continues not to win titles in the face of Hakkinen-style surprises? And who will get the blame?

Despite recent failures, Michael remains the yardstick for other drivers and he desperately wants to prove as much.

After three seasons of loyal and true service in Michael Schumacher's shadow, Eddie Irvine finally stepped into the spotlight during the first race of the season. But will circumstances allow him to do that again?

Formula 1's most famous number two finally had a true taste of success on the Melbourne podium. If such euphoria continues, the Northern Irishman will doubtless enjoy it to the maximum.

Number

Ferrari

4 Eddie Irvine

Date and place of birth:	10 November 1965, Newtownards, Northern Ireland
Nationality:	British
Lives in:	Dublin (Ireland), Oxford (England) and Conlig (Northern Ireland)
Marital status:	single
Height/Weight:	1.78m/70kg
Hobbies:	golf, surfing, angling, flying his plane and helicopter
Favourite food and drink:	Chinese meals, beer
First race:	Japan 1993 (Jordan)
F1 statistics:	4th in 1998 (Ferrari). 82 starts, 119 points, 1 win, 0 pole positions
F1 record:	**1993**: One point in two starts with Jordan-Hart. **1994**: Jordan-Hart. 14th in the championship with 6pts. **1995**: Jordan-Peugeot. 12th, 10pts. **1996**: Ferrari. 10th, 11pts. **1997**: Ferrari. 7th, 24pts. **1998**: Ferrari. 4th, 47pts. **1999**: Ferrari. Led championship after winning the opening race.

Eddie is good. On the streets of Melbourne, he laid to rest the bad boy reputation of his early days.

Rather than being head boy at Jordan he chose to become Schumacher's personal manservant at Ferrari. But he has at last been able to show he knows how to win races and can thus dream of boundless glory and a team leader's salary. So it's not all bad news. As many have pointed out (with varying degrees of sincerity, admittedly), "There's nothing dishonourable about living in the shadow of a Senna or a Schumacher."

And so Irvine is quite content and, from his point of view, can't see why more drivers wouldn't accept his situation. But doesn't he ever wonder what it would be like to lead a team such as Jordan, and have the authority to dictate how things are done? He has free rein to race as he pleases on very rare occasions – i.e. only when his team leader has been knocked out of contention. Hence his maiden win in the 1999 Australian GP. That day he wiped away three years of

bitterness (and criticism). But let there be no illusions. If he was to strike out on his own in the face of the wishes of his team-mate and his employer, he would quickly be removed to make way for someone of the calibre of Jarno Trulli and Mika Salo. Such drivers are still making their way in Formula One,

and might be willing to accept the required level of subservience. But that hasn't happened yet. If such rivalry were to occur it would indicate that the Scuderia was capable of winning every race and that Irvine had stolen a march on Schumacher in terms of pure speed. We are a long way from that.

Frank Williams and Patrick Head have started with a clean sheet. They are relying on Ralf Schumacher and Alessandro Zanardi to get them back on the right track.

The first true "post-Newey" Williams, will the FW21 really enable the team to forget about its departed design guru's move to Woking?

Supertec FB 01
(né Renault-Mécachrome)
71-degree V10
Capacity not disclosed
Length: 623mm
Width: 542mm
Height: 395mm
Weight: 120kg

Address:	Williams Engineering Ltd, Grove, Wantage, Oxon OX12 0DQ, England
Tel:	(44) 0123 577 7700
Fax:	(44) 0123 576 4705
Internet:	www.icnsportsweb.com
Number of staff:	260
First GP:	Spain 1969 (as entrant, with Brabham chassis); Argentina 1975 (as Williams)
GP starts:	392 (332 since 75)
Wins:	103
First win:	Britain 1979 (Clay Regazzoni)
Poles:	108
Fastest laps:	109
Points scored:	1960.5 (av. per GP since 75: 5.90)
World constructors' titles:	9 (80, 81, 86, 87, 92, 93, 94, 96, 97)
World drivers' titles:	7 (Jones 80, Rosberg 82, Piquet 87, Mansell 92, Prost 93, D. Hill 96, J. Villeneuve 97)
Test driver:	Jörg Müller (Germany)
1998 record:	3rd (38pts)

Managing director:
Frank Williams

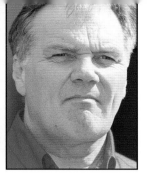

Technical director:
Patrick Head

• Plus points
Refreshed driver line-up
Completely new car
Fierce desire to avenge last year's relative
 failure

• Minus points
Zanardi needs to reacclimatise to F1
Ralf Schumacher's temperament
Will the FW21 be good enough?

SUPERTEC Williams

Williams FW21 – Tyres Bridgestone

Even though Williams has commenced its new technical partnership with BMW in the factory, on the track it will be very much a year of transition.

There is no doubt that the 1998 season left a bitter taste in the mouths of Frank Williams and Patrick Head. Accustomed to fighting at the head of the field, they found it a extraordinarily humbling experience to be fighting for "only" third place in the constructors' championship.

As a result, they headed to the USA to find the spark they believed would spur their revival. Capable, combative F1 returnee Alex Zanardi will certainly need time to adapt, but he comes equipped with the experience, fighting spirit and technical touch Williams needs to give it a lift. To

accompany the cool, polished Italian, the men from Grove have called on the youthful fire of the younger Schumacher. Gifted and belligerent in equal measure (some see in him elements of Nigel Mansell), he has a glorious opportunity to give his career a massive boost.

Once he has taken time to readjust, Alessandro Zanardi should be able to reward the immense faith that others have in him. He dominated the past two seasons in America's premier Champ Car series.

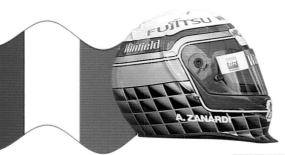

Date and place of birth:	23 October 1966, Bologna, Italy
Nationality:	Italian
Lives in:	Monte Carlo
Marital status:	married to Daniela, son Niccolo
Height/Weight:	1.76m/71kg
Hobbies :	skiing, tennis, mountain biking and gymnasium work
First race:	Spain 1991 (Jordan)
F1 statistics:	20th in 1993 (Lotus). 25 starts, 1 point, 0 wins, 0 pole positions
F1 record:	**1991**: Debut with Jordan. 9th in Spain and Australia. **1992**: Benetton test driver. 3 races for Minardi as substitute for Christian Fittipaldi. **1993**: Lotus-Ford. 6th in Brazil. Massive accident in Belgium – out of racing for four months. 20th in the championship with 1pt. **1994**: Lotus-Ford. Test driver, then called up to replace Pedro Lamy after the Monaco GP. 9th in Spain, but then dropped for last two races of the year. (**1997/1998**: Indycar champion with Ganassi Racing. 11 wins.) **1999**: Williams-Supertec.

Number **5**

Williams

Alessandro Zanardi

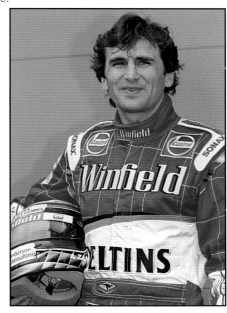

Alex Zanardi's career has taken a curious route. It was a minor triumph in itself that he escaped without injury from his frightening accident during practice for the 1993 Belgian GP, when the active suspension of his Lotus failed. But he didn't get to taste real success until later, when he opted for a period of American exile. Over there, no one could cope with his desire to prove himself, nor his aggression and talent. He made his name and fortune with successive Indycar titles and was faced with the choice of staying on or coming back to Europe. The combination of (then) forthcoming fatherhood and the chance to move to one of the best F1 teams persuaded him to return to his cultural roots.

Will it be too long before we see him on the podium? In the five years he has been away, F1 has evolved and is now as far removed from what Zanardi knew before as it is from Champ Car racing. And so

Alex has to relearn his craft, to work out how to brake at the limit on rock hard tyres, to follow a single racing line to the centimetre, to play around with settings and to place as much trust in his engineer's deductions as he does in computer read-outs. It's a different job, all right. And it's made all the more difficult by the fact that the

1999 Williams seems little more effective than its predecessor. But once he has found his feet again, Alex can put his concerns to one side and look ahead to next year's Williams-BMW. Nice as it is to see him back, however, this is no cushy number. And there's always the chance that Ralf Schumacher will prove a tough nut to crack.

Warm and outgoing, Alex has already won over the paddock. Now he needs to do the same to the stopwatch...

33

After a two-year apprenticeship at Jordan, the younger Schumacher today finds himself in a position to win grands prix. A top three finish in Australia ensured a dazzling start to his Williams career. No question, he has the world at his feet.

Although his car is still short of development, Ralf managed to work his way onto the podium in Melbourne. From his personal viewpoint that was a great result.

Date and place of birth:	30 June 1975, Hürth, Germany
Nationality:	German
Lives in:	Monte Carlo
Marital status:	single
Height/Weight:	1.78m/73kg
Hobbies:	karting, tennis, cycling, and backgammon
Favourite food and drink:	Italian cuisine, apple juice with mineral water
First race:	Australia 1997 (Jordan)
F1 statistics:	10th in 1998 (Jordan). 34 starts, 41 points, 0 wins, 0 pole positions
F1 record:	**1997**: Jordan-Peugeot. 3rd in Argentina. 11th in the championship with 13pts. **1998**: Jordan-Mugen-Honda. 2nd in Belgium. 10th, 14pts. **1999**: Williams-Supertec. 3rd in Australia.

Number 6

Williams
Ralf Schumacher

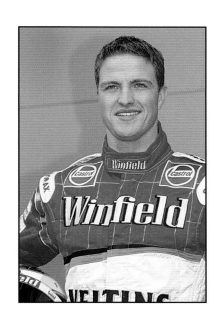

Is he as gifted as his elder brother? There are some that believe so. Certainly, last season at Jordan Damon Hill found it tough to prove otherwise. And that could give Zanardi something to worry about. What is known is that Ralf is not so talented out of the cockpit, particularly when it comes to dealing with other people. Alongside him, Patrick Head comes over as a positive livewire, the life and soul of the party. It has to be said that with his surname, a high-profile brother in the next pit and Willi Weber as his manager, it wasn't going to take long before he established his character, though not necessarily in the best way... That being so, why did Sir Frank Williams sign him up? Was it simply that, being unable to have the real thing, he was happy with an impressive copy?

Whatever, BMW and Germany's press, TV and race fans are over the moon. A little untidy when he started, a situation not aided by his uneasy relationship with Fisichella, Ralf Schumacher has matured technically. If he can match that with determination and psychological fortitude there is no doubt that Williams will give him the backing he needs. The only doubt concerns his ability to deal with a team that is loath to pamper its drivers and prefers to develop its car to suit the thinking of its designers rather than the man behind the wheel. For Schumacher Jnr, this season is just as important a career stage as it is for Zanardi. It will be a good measure of his real potential.

Determined and psychologically strong, Ralf could be tailor-made for the Williams team.

After having placed its faith in youth for many seasons, the Jordan team has opted this time for experience in the form of Hill and Frentzen – a solid combination.

Having slipped out of Williams via the back door, Frentzen marked his Jordan entrance in grand style during the Australian Grand Prix. He is determined to repair his reputation this year.

Mugen-Honda MF301HD V10
Capacity not disclosed
Length: 625mm
Width: 525mm
Height: 470mm
Weight not disclosed

Address:	Jordan Grand Prix, Silverstone, Northamptonshire NN12 8TJ, England
Tel:	(44) 0132 785 7153
Fax:	(44) 0132 785 2120
Internet:	www.jordangp.com
Number of staff:	150
First GP:	America 1991
GP starts:	130
Points scored:	155 (average per GP: 1.19)
Wins:	1 (Belgium 1998)
Poles:	1
Fastest laps:	2
Best result in constructors' championship:	4th in 1998
Test driver:	Shinji Nakano (Japan)
1998 record:	4th (34pts)

Managing director:
Eddie Jordan

Technical director:
Mike Gascoyne

• **Plus points**
Heading in the right direction
Extra finance available
Experienced drivers
A powerful, reliable engine

• **Minus points**
Frentzen might need time to adapt
Possible driver rivalry
Mike Gascoyne's ultimate potential as yet unknown

MUGEN-HONDA
Jordan

Jordan 199 – Tyres Bridgestone

Hot on the heels of Damon Hill's Spa win last season, the Jordan team wants to maintain its progress and finish among the top three constructors in 1999.

The 1998 season added two essential elements to Jordan's armoury: a first victory and a so far unseen level of expectation for the future. Galvanised by its first win and knowing that it now has the ability to compete with the "Big Four" in F1, the team has set itself fresh standards. In order to achieve them, Eddie Jordan – the driving force – has completely revised his set-up and his approach. He doesn't just want to be strong technically; he wants to be strong financially. To that end he has sold a 40 per cent stake of the business to American investment group Warburg Pincus. And thanks to the injection of new capital he has been able to strengthen the team as it faces up to the new millennium. He's sure that the next decade will belong to him and he has made sweeping changes in order to prepare what he hopes will be a title challenge. After 10 years together, Eddie and his long-standing technical director Gary Anderson were both ready for fresh pastures. The former linked up with ex-Tyrrell designer Mike Gascoyne, the latter headed for a new job with Stewart.

Damon Hill has struck up a perfect partnership with Mike Gascoyne, Jordan's new technical director. Rivals be warned: these two could cause a few surprises this season.

After giving Irishman Eddie Jordan's team its first victory last season, Damon Hill now wants to help propel them into the championship's top three. It's a challenge well within the grasp of Britain's former champion, who remains as enthusiastic as ever.

Date and place of birth:	17 September 1960, London, England
Nationality:	British
Lives in:	Dublin, Ireland
Marital status:	married to Georgie, four children (Oliver, Joshua, Tabatha and Rosy)
Height/Weight:	1.82m/70kg
Hobbies:	motorbikes, skiing, golf, tennis, music and playing the guitar
Favourite food and drink:	home-made pasta, beer and wine
First race:	Britain 1992 (Brabham)
F1 statistics:	World champion in 1996 (Williams). 101 starts, 353 points, 22 wins, 20 pole positions
F1 record:	**1992**: Brabham-Judd. Test driver for Williams. **1993**: Williams-Renault. 1st win at Budapest, plus two others at Spa and Monza. 3rd in the championship with 39pts. **1994**: Williams-Renault. 6 wins, 2 poles. 2nd, 91pts. BBC Sports Personality of the Year. **1995**: Williams-Renault. 4 wins, 7 poles, 6 accidents! 2nd, 69pts. **1996**: Williams-Renault. 8 wins, 9 poles. World champion, 97pts. **1997**: Arrows-Yamaha. 2nd in Hungary. 12th, 7pts. **1998**: Jordan-Mugen-Honda. Won in Belgium. 6th, 20pts. **1999**: Jordan-Mugen-Honda.

Number 7

Jordan - Mugen - Honda

Damon Hill

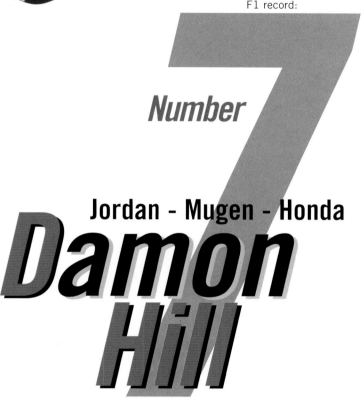

Although he is now 38, the 1996 world champion still craves victory.

Williams made him, turning him from an anonymous test driver into a world champion who is a hero to British race fans. And Williams also dismissed him without ceremony, on the day his manager set his financial demands too high. The world champion was slung out into the wilderness – and when Arrows picked him up he was unable to turn their fortunes around. It appeared to show that Frank's judgment was not the least eccentric. No matter, Damon had made his fortune...and continued to do so when Jordan picked him up, and gave him a new lease of life at the age of 38. Although he is oldest man in the field, he does not have the race experience of some contemporaries. He has something of a privileged status, thanks to his past achievements and to his role as Jordan's first-ever GP winner, and with his current team he has found a level of support sometimes lacking in the past. Even if Ralf Schumacher was a disruptive influence...

This season he has to put up with the man chosen as his replacement by Williams, a man whose form in Australia implied he will keep Damon on his toes. Very quick when everything is working well, a reliable finisher and with plenty of technical ability, Damon will doubtless have a number of surprises in store for us this season. Assuming that Frentzen doesn't stoke up too many old demons. Remember the number of mistakes that were made in the old days, when he had Schumacher glued under his rear wing?

Rediscover the taste of victory – it's just what Heinz-Harald Frentzen wants to do at the dawn of a new season that will be decisive for the Jordan team. He quickly reacclimatised to its convivial modus operandi (he last drove for Eddie in 1990, in the European F3000 series) and had a successful start to his campaign in Melbourne.

Second place in Australia got Frentzen's season off to a promising start. With his growing maturity he wants to prove to the world that the team belongs up there with the best of them.

Date and place of birth:	18 May 1967, Mönchengladbach, Germany
Nationality:	German
Lives in:	Monte Carlo
Marital status:	single, lives with Tanja
Height/Weight:	1.78m/74.5kg
Hobbies:	karting, boating and model aeroplanes
Favourite food and drink:	his mum's paella, grilled fish, pâté, fruit juice
First race:	Brazil 1994 (Sauber)
F1 statistics:	2nd in 1997 (Williams). 81 starts, 94 points, 1 win, 1 pole position
F1 record:	**1994**: Sauber-Mercedes. 4th in France, 5th in the Pacific GP, 6th in the European and Japanese GPs. 13th in the championship with 7pts. **1995**: Sauber-Ford. 1st podium, Monza. 9th, 15pts. **1996**: Sauber-Ford, 12th, 7pts. **1997**: Williams-Renault. First win at Imola, first pole in Monaco. 2nd, 42pts. **1998**: Williams-Mécachrome. 7th, 17pts. **1999**: Jordan-Mugen-Honda. 2nd in Australia.

Number

8

Jordan - Mugen - Honda

Heinz-Harald Frentzen

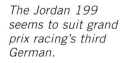

Peter Sauber had blind faith in his ability. Frank Williams employed him because he believed here was the only driver who could beat Schumacher, Frentzen's eternal rival. And not just on the track: the current Mrs Schumacher is a former companion of Frentzen's. But a failed romance was nothing compared to subsequent on-track disappointments. And his downfall at Williams was the cruellest blow because he was passed over for another German as the team's relationship with BMW got into its stride. That was hard to swallow.

Frentzen is certainly a skilful driver, but he also has a taste for an easy life – and the two don't mix. Being gifted is not enough. You have to cultivate your talents and improve them. Williams does not tolerate the ruminations of amateur philosophers: remember the awkward collaboration between Jones and Reutemann in the early Eighties? The fact is that Frentzen did not respond at the heart of a top-class team. But just as he was about to head for the United States to begin a new career (against his will), he opted instead for Jordan. And that was a move supported, it is said, by Bernie Ecclestone, who wants to maintain a high level of interest for TV viewers in Germany. The open spirit of this still young team and the accessibility of new technical director Mike Gascoyne will be perfectly suited to this untypical German. (Frentzen is half-Spanish, and the only Teutonic thing about him is his passport.) Why did everyone want to turn him into the anti-Schumacher? Quite simply, it's because they thought he could do it. Matured by age and adversity, he now understands as much. And he has the respect of his colleagues. 1999 is an important year. It gives Frentzen a chance to obliterate a couple of painful memories.

The Jordan 199 seems to suit grand prix racing's third German.

43

Benetton
Formula 1
RACING TEAM

Though Benetton might have been touched by a little Aboriginal spirit, it is placing greater faith this season in the spirit of youth. With Fisichella and Wurz Benetton's United Colors should soon be flying again.

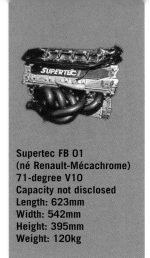

**Supertec FB 01
(né Renault-Mécachrome)
71-degree V10
Capacity not disclosed
Length: 623mm
Width: 542mm
Height: 395mm
Weight: 120kg**

Address:	Benetton Formula One Racing Team, Whiteways Technical Centre, Enstone, Chipping Norton, Oxon OX7 4EE, England
Tel:	(44) 0160 867 8000
Fax:	(44) 0160 867 8609
Internet:	www.jnet.ad.jp
Number of staff:	205
First GP:	San Marino 1981 (as Toleman); Brazil 1986 (as Benetton)
GP starts:	267 (210 since 86)
Wins:	27
First win:	Mexico 1986 (Gerhard Berger)
Poles:	16
Fastest laps:	35
Points scored:	831.5 (average per GP: 3.01)
World constructors' titles:	1 (95)
World drivers' titles:	2 (M. Schumacher 94, 95)
Test driver:	Laurent Redon (France)
1998 record:	5th (33pts)

Managing director:
Rocco Benetton

Technical director:
Pat Symonds

• **Plus points**
Calm has been restored
Two good drivers
Imaginative design chief

• **Minus points**
Reduced funding
No tie to a major manufacturer
Reliability as yet unproven

SUPERTEC
Benetton

Benetton B199 – Tyres Bridgestone

After several seasons of instability, Benetton has been restructured around a young, ambitious boss. Will Rocco Benetton be the man to lead the renaissance?

I t's transformation time: from restraint there comes adventure and stormy waters now appear calm. Internal bickering and a conservative engineering approach have marked the past two years, but now Benetton is back on the attack. Weakened by recent goings-on, the team has taken stock and restructured; power is now back in the hands of the family from which the company takes its name. Rocco and his brothers have tidied up the shop and breathed fresh spirit into the business.

On the technical side, there are several new ideas from design chief Nick Wirth, a man it is sometimes difficult to pigeonhole. One of these has already been given plenty of column inches in the press: the FTT (Front Torque Transfer) system. This was tested in private last year and is a means of distributing the load between the front brakes to prevent lock-up. If it helps braking, it might just assist the thorny problem of overtaking, a rare art in Formula One. Could this be the something extra that makes the difference?

In 1998 Giancarlo Fisichella came of age. He was head and shoulders ahead of his team-mate and he also showed good tactical awareness when he finished second in Monaco and Canada. For him, 1999 is a key season in which he wants to improve on last year's efforts.

Surrounded by a team that has settled down at last, Giancarlo can look ahead to a bright season. He justified expectations with a strong drive to fourth place in the first race of the year.

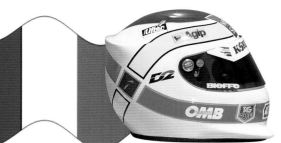

Number

Benetton - Supertec
Giancarlo Fisichella

Date and place of birth:	14 January 1973, Rome, Italy
Nationality:	Italian
Lives in:	Monte Carlo
Marital status:	married to Luna, first child due soon
Height/Weight:	1.72m/68kg
Hobbies:	tennis, football, mountain biking, fishing and skiing
Favourite food and drink:	pasta, orange juice and Coca-Cola
First race:	Australia 1996 (Minardi)
F1 statistics:	8th in 1997 (Jordan). 42 starts, 36 points, 0 wins, 1 pole position
F1 record:	**1996**: Minardi-Ford. Selected races.

1997: Jordan-Peugeot. 8th in the championship with 20pts.
1998: Benetton-Mécachrome. 9th, 16pts. **1999**: Benetton-Supertec. 4th in the opening GP.

The B199 seems to suit Fisichella. He believes the car has great potential and is enthusiastic about the new FTT (Front Torque Transfer) braking system.

Fisico has risen meteorically through professional motorsport, under the guiding hand of mentor Flavio Briatore. Having shown Ralf Schumacher what he was made of when they were at Jordan, he is now marking his time. And that's a pity, because he's not the torpid type, far from it. Last year he held his own against his young, effervescent team-mate Wurz. He didn't score more points, but he did gain an edge by getting stuck into the thick of the battle more frequently. What does it all mean?

The truth is that Fisichella came to a good team at a bad time. After losing Michael Schumacher, key engineers Brawn and Byrne and two team directors (Briatore and David Richards) in quick succession, Benetton had fallen from its perch. Its lack of structural stability had weakened

the business. Worse, about £12 million had to be found from somewhere for a Supertec engine contract. Sensitive to his surroundings, as all Latins are, Fisichella went through a quiet patch. Now his potential is known, however, and his future achievements hinge on the performance of the Benetton B199. Whatever happens, it won't be for want of trying.

Coming into his second full season in F1, the bright, steady Austrian needs to show that he can match his spirited Italian team-mate for speed. His consistency has earned him the respect of his team, but he needs to add fire and conviction to his performances if he is fight on equal terms with Fisichella.

Australia 1999 wasn't a race to remember for Alexander and he retired at the end of an unhappy weekend. Outpaced once again by Giancarlo, he failed to get among the pace-setters.

Date and place of birth:	15 February 1974, Waidhofen/Thaya, Austria
Nationality:	Austrian
Lives in:	Monte Carlo
Marital status:	engaged to Karin
Height/Weight:	1.86m/82.4kg
Hobbies:	skiing, snowboarding, mountain biking and squash
Favourite food and drink:	pasta, apple juice with mineral water
First race:	Canada 1997 (Benetton)
F1 statistics:	Equal 7th in 1998 (Benetton). 20 starts, 21 points, 0 wins, 0 pole positions
F1 record:	**1997**: Test driver for Benetton-Renault. Started 3 races as substitute for injured Gerhard Berger. 14th in the championship with 4pts. **1998**: Benetton-Mécachrome. Equal 7th, 17pts. **1999**: Benetton-Supertec.

Number 10
Alexander Wurz
Benetton - Supertec

Barring accidents in the 1999 season, Alexander Wurz can hope to polish up his skills at the wheel of the B199.

Another Flavio Briatore discovery! Not helped physically by his great height, this young Austrian showed great potential when he was called up for three races in 1997, after compatriot Gerhard Berger had been laid low by a dental infection. This brief flash of promise was enough to earn him a place in the race team when Berger decided to retire at the end of that season. He has no hang-ups at all about Fisichella and he has already made his mark on several occasions – not always in the way he would have wished.

His barrel roll at the start of the Canadian GP in 1998 ought to have calmed his approach a little (though he still finished fourth in the restarted race). Like Fisichella, he won't be blamed if Benetton fails to deliver this season. He has already proved his mettle.

More effort than ever before has gone into creating the latest Sauber racer. Will that be enough to make it the team's first winner?

Red Bull
SAUBER PETRONAS

It's as important a season for Pedro Diniz as it is for his new Swiss team. His target is to rid himself, once and for all, of his image as a mere "rentadriver".

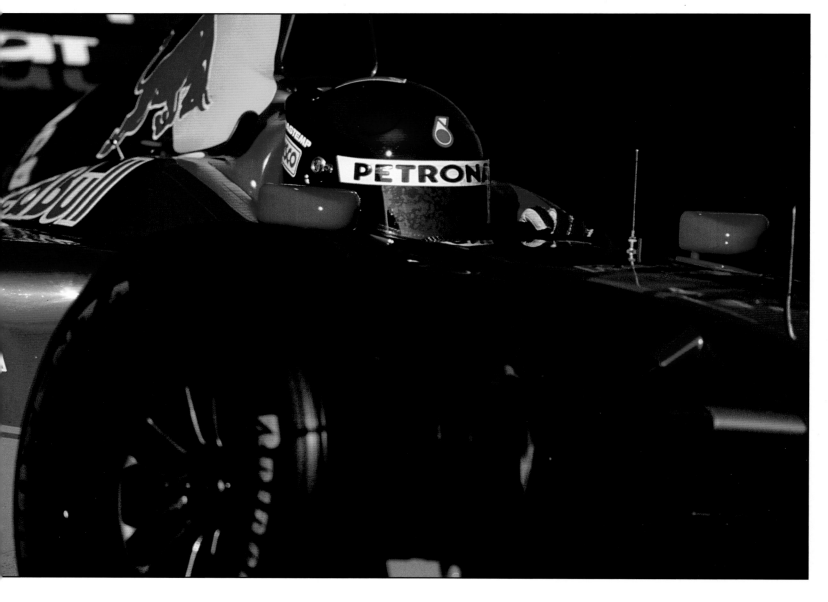

**Petronas SPE 03A
(né Ferrari)
80-degree V10
Capacity: 2997cc
Dimensions not disclosed
Weight not disclosed**

Address:	P.P. Sauber AG,
	Wildbach Strasse 9,
	CH-8340 Hinwil, Switzerland
Tel:	00 41 1938 14 00
Fax:	00 41 1938 16 80
Internet:	www.redbull-sauber.ch
Number of staff:	150
First GP:	South Africa 1993
GP starts:	97
Points scored:	90 (average per GP: 0.92)
Best result in	
constructors' championship:	6th in 98
Test driver:	TBA
98 record:	6th (10pts)

Managing director:
Peter Sauber

Technical director:
Leo Ress

• **Plus points**
Alesi's fighting spirit
A balanced driver line-up
Ferrari V10

• **Minus points**
The R&D department could do with a lift
Team relies on self-sufficiency

PETRONAS Sauber

Sauber C18 – Tyres Bridgestone

After six years in F1, the Sauber team must move on. It has picked up points and podiums in the past – but now it needs to start winning.

Peter Sauber makes no bones about it: his team has been in Formula One for six years now – and with that kind of experience it is time to take the next step forward. The Swiss team has points and podium finishes to its credit. Now it wants to taste victory – and if that's a realistic aim then why not dream of a world title bid, too? The Hinwil team believes it has two vital assets as it seeks to realise its ambitions. One is a proven engine: the Ferrari V10 used by Schumacher and Irvine from the 1998 Italian GP on. The other is a redoubtable competitor. Last year, the spirit of Jean Alesi entranced a Sauber crew that has all too often been stuck in a rut. The team was motivated as much by his sharp tongue as it was by his enthusiasm. Peter Sauber has chosen Pedro Diniz to partner the mercurial Frenchman. Dedicated and skilful, the São Paulo native has an opportunity to get rid, once and for all, of his reputation as a mere "rentadriver".

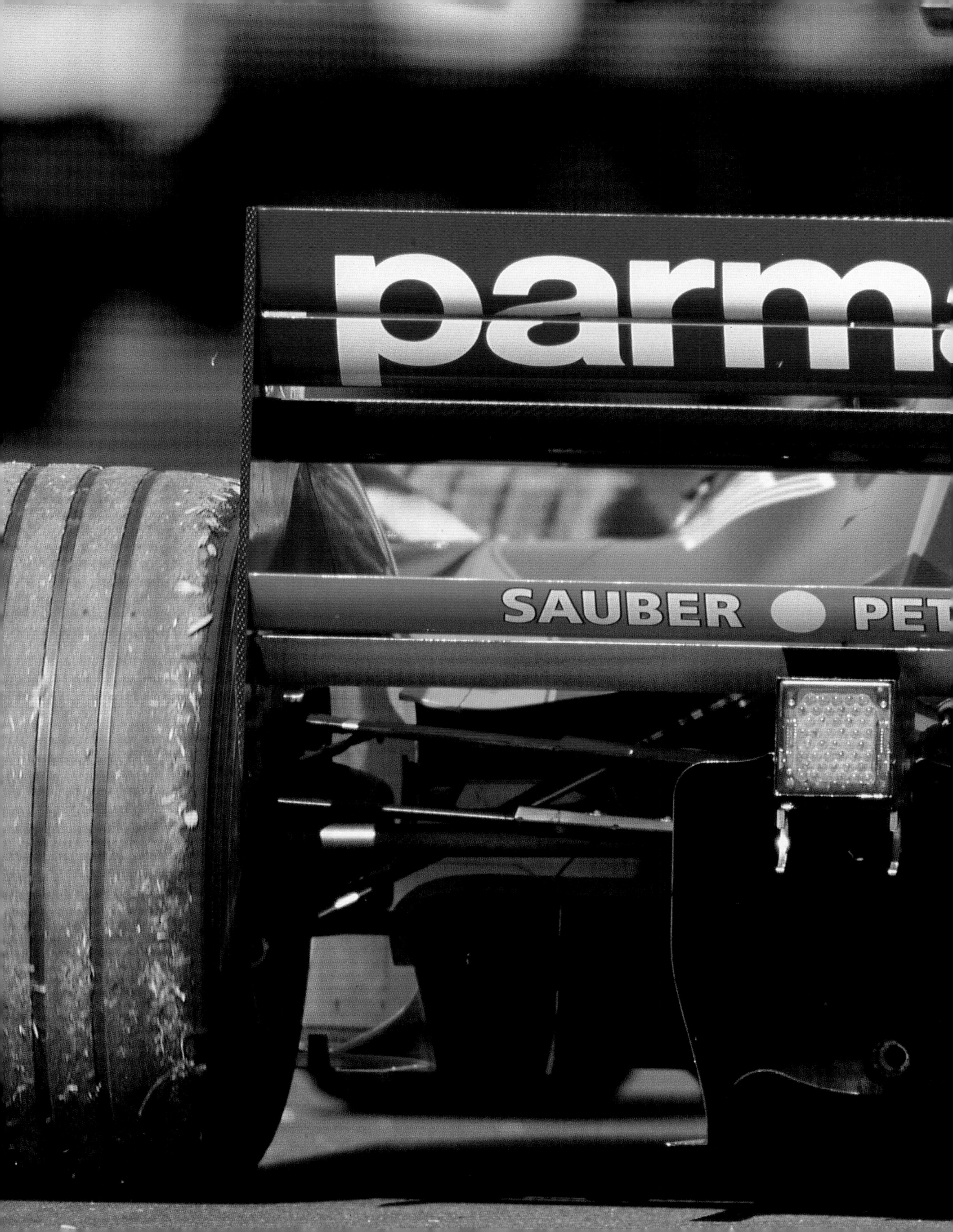
SAUBER

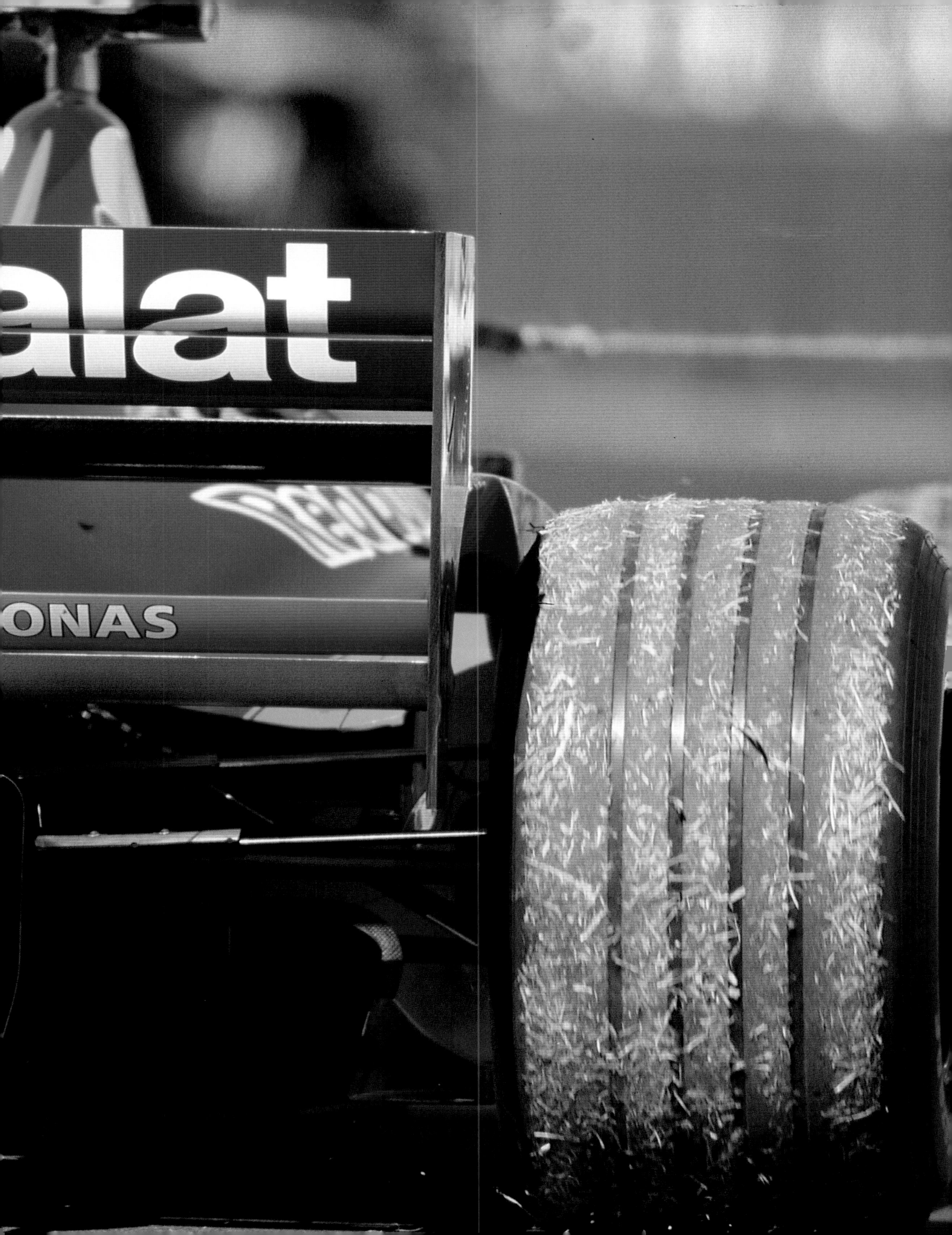
alat
ONAS

The doyen of modern F1 drivers enters another new season with the firm intention of conjuring up more of the inspirational drives for which he is renowned. Surrounded by a team that adores him, Jean Alesi hopes to leave enough of a mark on the season that it will lead him, perhaps, to brighter, better things...

When fired up, the emotional French driver knows how to convey his enthusiasm to members of the Swiss team that has been, until now, a little too cut off. But Jean has kindled the ambition of everyone in Hinwil.

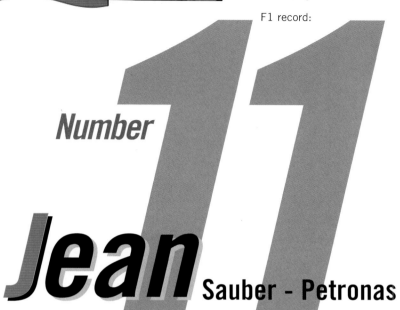

Date and place of birth:	11 June 1964, Avignon, France
Nationality:	French
Lives in:	Nyon, Switzerland
Marital status:	divorced, lives with Kumiko; daughters Charlotte and Elena
Height/Weight:	1.70m/72kg
Hobbies:	family, gym work, Nordic skiing, jogging and mountaineering
Favourite food and drink:	pasta, mineral water
First race:	France 1989 (Tyrrell)
F1 statistics:	4th in 1996 and 1997 (Benetton). 152 starts, 225 points, 1 win, 2 pole positions
F1 record:	**1989**: Part-season with Tyrrell-Ford. 9th in the championship with 8pts. **1990**: Tyrrell-Ford. 9th, 13pts. **1991**: Ferrari. 7th, 21pts. **1992**: Ferrari, 7th, 18pts. **1993**: Ferrari. 6th, 16pts. **1994**: Ferrari. 5th, 24pts. **1995**: Ferrari. First win in Canada. 5th, 42pts. **1996**: Benetton-Renault. 4th, 47pts. **1997**: Benetton-Renault. 4th, 36pts. **1998**: Sauber-Petronas. 11th, 9pts. **1999**: Sauber-Petronas.

Number 11
Jean Alesi
Sauber - Petronas

Alesi is the most experienced grand prix driver racing today. But he doesn't make a fuss about it, which is typical. He is still hungry for success – and not just because he has won only a single race to date. During five years with Ferrari he wowed the tifosi, carved himself a reputation and made his fortune – but he didn't come out of it with a glittering CV. He saw a succession of team managers, engineers and consultants come and go, he witnessed several attempts to restructure the team...then when everything was finally in place to take the team forward he was passed over in favour of Michael Schumacher. There is no place for sentiment in F1, though Alesi still has a genuine soft spot for the Scuderia. Although he was expected to wreak his revenge when he joined Benetton, that turned out to be just another downward step. The team was in chaos following Schumacher's departure, and Alesi was a convenient scapegoat. But

he's put those two seasons behind him. Jean Alesi is back on top form at the epicentre of a team bereft of the petty politics and personal differences that can have a detrimental effect on confidence and performance.

Unfortunately, Sauber is not a top-level team. It has a customer engine, which is expensive, and the money that takes could be well invested on other things. And is

Sauber's R&D team up to the standards demanded by F1? Even so, Alesi has committed heart and soul to a project that has refreshed his enthusiasm, even though it cannot bring him the results and rewards his experience and talents deserve. Good results could set him on course for another team, perhaps one better equipped to challenge for wins. And one which is nearer to the rest of the racing community.

With a kick from the powerful, Ferrari-derived Petronas engine, Jean Alesi has set himself higher targets this season.

Pedro Diniz has had more than enough of hearing people say he only got to F1 because of his bank balance. After having given Damon Hill a run for his money at Arrows, he compared favourably to Mika Salo last year – and now he wants to reinforce his reputation alongside Alesi at Sauber.

The latest recruit to Switzerland's F1 team got of to a flying start. In Melbourne he proved he has already settled in well by outqualifying his team-mate.

Date and place of birth:	22 May 1970, São Paulo, Brazil
Nationality:	Brazilian
Lives in:	Monte Carlo and São Paulo
Marital status:	single
Height/Weight:	1.74m/68kg
Hobbies :	reading, water sports, skiing (downhill and Nordic), cycling and squash
Favourite food and drink:	pasta, water
First race:	Brazil 1995 (Forti)
F1 statistics:	13th in 1998 (Arrows). 67 starts, 7 points, 0 wins, 0 pole positions
F1 record:	**1995**: Forti-Ford. No points. **1996**: Ligier-Mugen-Honda. 15th in the championship with 2pts. **1997**: Arrows-Yamaha. 17th, 2pts. **1998**: Arrows-TWR. 13th, 3pts. **1999**: Sauber-Petronas.

Number 12

Sauber - Petronas

Pedro Diniz

On a mission to prove himself, Pedro Diniz could be one of the revelations of the season.

Alesi and Diniz: two drivers who were made for each other. The former has suffered with a reputation as a rock ape who spends more time in the gravel traps than on the track. The latter has been dismissed as a playboy who is in F1 only because he has a lot more sponsorship than ability. True, his backing helped him to scorch through the junior formulae without having to worry about his results or spend time vegetating in moderate teams, but Diniz has nonetheless stunned the F1 world with his rate of progress.

Reliable, diligent, a good test driver, a fine PR man and with a physique fit for anything, the Brazilian has proved he deserves his place among the elite for reasons other then the £4.5 million budget he brings with him. He proved that he had nothing to be ashamed of against celebrated team-mates such as Damon Hill (in 1997) and Mika Salo (last year).

"He'd be better out of F1," said Flavio Briatore when he worked with Diniz at Ligier. Sauber hasn't made the same mistake, however.

He won't threaten Alesi's number one status, as Herbert did in 1998, and he will certainly pick up a few precious points. Diniz is a true sportsman who seeks only to prove himself as an F1 driver – and to enjoy himself in the process. He is the last of a breed of gentleman drivers that, generally speaking, vanished from F1 a long time ago.

A revised version of 1998's A20 chassis, the latest racer from Leafield could surprise a few people this season. It did just that by scoring a point in Melbourne.

**Arrows-F1
80-degree V10
Capacity: 2997cc
Dimensions not disclosed
Weight not disclosed**

Address:	Arrows GP International, Leafield Technical Centre, Leafield, nr Witney, Oxon OX8 5PF, England
Tel:	(44) 0199 387 1000
Fax:	(44) 0199 387 1100
Internet:	www.arrows.com
Number of staff:	170
First GP:	Brazil 1978
GP starts:	304
Points scored:	156 (average per GP: 0.51)
Best result in constructors' championship:	4th in 1988
Test driver:	TBA
1998 record:	7th (6pts)

Managing Director:
Tom Walkinshaw

Joint-owner:
Malik Ado Ibrahim

• **Plus points**
Extra funding available
Engine has made progress
Solid technical base

• **Minus points**
Drivers short of experience
Still searching for an alliance with a mainstream
 manufacturer
Low-key image

Arrows

Arrows A20 – Tyres Bridgestone

On the edge of a financial precipice last season, the Arrows team staged something of a recovery during the winter. For 1999, the target is to prepare for a prosperous future.

The big news of the winter was the sale of Arrows to a consortium comprising Tom Walkinshaw, Nigerian Prince Malik Ado Ibrahim and an investment group belonging to merchant bank Morgan Grenfell. Although the injection of fresh capital was enough to wipe out reported debts of almost £20 million, it wasn't enough to prevent an evacuation in the engineering department. With former design chief John Barnard having opted for a new role at Prost GP, his former assistant Mike Coughlan now heads the technical staff.

Throughout the winter the team has focused on developing the Hart-designed V10 engine, in a quest to find a cure for last season's reliability problems. This is the only team apart from Ferrari to put its own name to an engine. The difference, however, is that Arrows' engine budget is reportedly about £20 million; in ohter words just one-sixth of that available to the famous Italian marque...

A refugee from the Tyrrell fold, Tora Takagi was a last-minute replacement for Mika Salo just a few days before teams set off for Australia. After a few tests Tom Walkinshaw finally offered him the Finn's seat, though it didn't exactly come free...

A protégé of Japan's Eighties racing star Satoru Nakajima, Takagi will find that Arrows is a good place to complete his F1 education. He has already shown considerable promise and a strong career beckons.

Date and place of birth:	12 February 1974, Shizuoka, Japan
Nationality:	Japanese
Lives in:	Shizuoka
Marital status:	single
Height/Weight:	1.80m/61kg
Hobbies:	karting and snowboarding
Favourite food and drink:	pasta, mineral water
First race:	Australia 1998 (Tyrrell)
F1 statistics:	Never classified. 16 starts, 0 points, 0 wins, 0 pole positions
F1 record:	**1998**: Tyrrell-Ford.
	1999: Arrows-TWR.

Number 14

Arrows
Toranosuke Takagi

No question, Takagi is the most promising young Japanese driver yet. If the equipment is up to the job, Tora is certainly capable of scoring points.

As far as speed is concerned, there's no problem. Takagi is quick. Perhaps even too much so sometimes, as the occasional rush of blood has led to some clumsy passing attempts. Still, it's often said that it's far easier to make a quick driver focused than it is to make a slow driver quick. Tom Walkinshaw has taken on that challenge – while hoping that the damage bill incurred by his new Japanese charge won't exceed the budget he brings with him. His interest in Takagi has to do with the longer term, however.

Does Arrows' future depend on a possible partnership with a major Japanese manufacturer, a company perhaps prepared to invest many millions of yen to have its name on the cylinder heads of Arrows' in-house engine? While waiting for something along these lines to take shape, Arrows must put up with at least one of Takagi's drawbacks – his aversion to speaking anything other than Japanese. In the briefing room there are always two extra chairs, on the pit wall two extra sets of headphones: one for Takagi's manager, ex-racer Satoru Nakajima, and one for his interpreter.

Winner in 1997 of the Formula Nippon title – Japan's equivalent of Formula 3000 – and Jordan test driver last season, Pedro de la Rosa spearheads the new wave of Spanish interest in F1.

The very least you can say of de la Rosa's F1 debut is that he didn't do a bad job. A solid drive yielded sixth place and gave the team a welcome point.

Date and place of birth:	24 February 1971, Barcelona, Spain
Nationality:	Spanish
Lives in:	Barcelona
Marital status:	single
Height/Weight:	1.78m/74kg
Hobbies:	karting, fishing, mountain biking, radio control models and Spanish pop music
Favourite food and drink:	pasta, water and fruit juice
First race:	Australia 1999 (Arrows)
F1 record:	**1999**: Arrows-TWR. F1 rookie.

Number 15

Arrows
Pedro de la Rosa

Despite his noble-sounding name, he is not a descendant of the Spanish aristocracy. (As is often Iberian custom, he took his mother's surname because he preferred it to his father's – Martinez.) After applying himself well last season in his role as Jordan test driver, a job for which his solid Repsol backing made him a most suitable candidate, he was hoping to partner Damon Hill this year. Political considerations subsequently favoured Frentzen, however. Jordan was still keen to hang on to its backing from the Spanish petrol company, but Tom Walkinshaw got the deal instead.

Throughout the winter de la Rosa pounded round Barcelona and Silverstone with monotonous regularity, but his lap times were respectable and he made few errors. But he still didn't know what his future held. "Being a test driver is a great job for a young driver," he says, "but it's also frustrating. I went to countless grands prix as a spectator, and found it hard to stay until Sunday. During my winter with Arrows I approached everything as though I was going to be doing the first race with them. And my work must have struck a chord. My only handicap is my lack of experience – but I'm mentally strong and physically in good shape, which will help." The presence of a second Spaniard in the field lends added spice because there is honour at stake. Throughout his career, however, de la Rosa has proved that he has the ability to achieve his goals.

Watch out for this quiet, thoughtful Spaniard who has finally obtained his F1 passport this season.

With Barrichello and Herbert on board, the team of Jackie and Paul Stewart has a strong, experienced driver line-up that could ruffle a few feathers this year.

Despite its still questionable reliability, the new Stewart-Ford SF-3 was a revelation on the streets of Melbourne. Arguably, it was fast enough to have won.

Ford CR-1
72-degree V10
Capacity: 2998cc
Length: 605mm
Width: 520mm
Height: 460mm

Address:	Stewart Grand Prix
	The Stewart Building, Brad Courne
	Drive, Tilbrook, Milton Keynes
	MK7 8BI, England
Tel:	(44) 0190 827 9794
Fax:	(44) 0190 827 9763
Internet:	www.stewartgp.com
Number of staff:	150
First GP:	Australia 1997
GP starts:	33
Points scored:	11 (average per GP: 0.33)
Best result in	
constructors' championship:	8th in 1998
Test driver:	TBA
1998 record:	8th (5pts)

Managing director:
Paul Stewart

Technical director:
Gary Anderson

• **Plus points**
The recruitment of Gary Anderson
Ford's will to win
Experienced drivers
Straightforward technical approach

• **Minus points**
Budget still tight
Question over reliability of latest
Ford V10

FORD
Stewart

Stewart SF-3 – Tyres Bridgestone

With a fresh management structure, a new technical director and extra Ford backing, Stewart could be the revelation of 1999.

New management structure, new technical director, new engine: Stewart Grand Prix shed its old skin prior to the most important season in its short history. Jackie Stewart's team acknowledges that it underachieved last season and knows it must make amends. At the launch of the Milton Keynes team's latest challenger, Stewart took the stage to deliver a simple, humble speech. To the point, it gave a detailed account of the important changes made during the winter. First of all, Scotland's three-time world champion said the time had come for him to take a step back and hand over presidency of the team to his son, Paul. It was not an announcement that signified his intention to retire, however, as Jackie will be focusing more than ever on furthering relations with current technical partners – and developing new associations. Also significant is the arrival from Jordan of the team's new technical director, Gary Anderson.

A mature racer has replaced the young "Rubinho" of the mid-Nineties. Rich in experience, he is now ready to take a leading role. His spirit is now free of Senna's memory, which haunted him for a long time.

Rubens made sparks fly in Melbourne. Forced to start from the pits after being hit by an engine problem on the grid, the Brazilian put in a storming recovery drive and picked up a couple of points for fifth place. If the Stewart can be made consistently reliable, Barrichello will be a serious victory candidate.

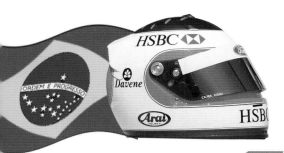

Date and place of birth:	23 May 1972, São Paulo, Brazil
Nationality:	Brazilian
Lives in:	Monte Carlo
Marital status:	married to Silvana
Height/Weight:	1.72m/79kg
Hobbies:	tennis, jogging, jet skiing and squash
Favourite food and drink:	pasta, diet Pepsi
First race:	South Africa 1993 (Jordan)
F1 statistics:	6th in 1994 (Jordan). 98 starts, 50 points, 0 wins, 1 pole position
F1 record:	**1993**: Jordan-Hart. 17th in the championship with 2pts.
	1994: Jordan-Hart. 6th, 19pts. **1995**: Jordan-Peugeot. 11th, 11pts.
	1996: Jordan-Peugeot. 8th, 14pts. **1997**: Stewart-Ford, 13th, 6pts.
	1998: Stewart-Ford.12th, 4pts. **1999**: Stewart-Ford.

Number 16

Stewart - Ford

Rubens Barrichello

Seven years in F1 and not a single result that reflects his true ability. That's hard to take. And it's not as if Barrichello hasn't had the opportunities. Unfortunately, severe depression and low morale marked those years that should have brought him his just deserts. Deeply affected by the loss of his friend and inspiration Ayrton Senna, it took him a long time to recover his equilibrium. And he also had to cope with pressure from the Brazilian media, who saw him as the natural successor to the late triple world champion. But, to his dismay, Barrichello was unable to deliver the goods.

Once four initially promising seasons with Jordan had led him nowhere, he took refuge with Stewart Grand Prix. The team needed building, the driver rebuilding. Solid results would be the best medicine, but the process would take a long time. By the end of 1998 we were beginning to wonder if it would ever happen,

though that had more to so with the engine supplier than the driver or the team. It's not easy to be confident about making the finish when you have 47 blow-ups in a season. But there is better news on the horizon after Ford decided to

take the bull by its horns. If the engine lasts, the Stewarts won't be far off the pace. Barrichello? He has to prove himself more effective than his richly experienced new team-mate if he wants to retain more than an outside chance.

With six years of F1 already under his belt, Barrichello is hungry for success. Will this be his year at last?

Old soldiers never die. Although he is one of the senior members of the grand prix field, the evergreen Johnny Herbert is always ready for battle.

Having transferred from Sauber, the Briton brings a wealth of solid technical experience to the young Stewart team. And they could also do with drawing on Johnny's inexhaustible reserves of good humour to put a smile back on their faces after a tough 1998.

Date and place of birth:	27 June 1964, Romford, England
Nationality:	British
Lives in:	Monte Carlo
Marital status:	married to Rebecca, two daughters
Height/Weight:	1.67m/65kg
Hobbies:	golf, cycling, gym work and radio control models
Favourite food and drink:	pasta, water
First race:	Brazil 1989 (Benetton)
F1 statistics:	4th in 1995 (Benetton). 129 starts, 83 points, 2 wins, 0 pole positions

F1 record: **1989**: Benetton-Ford then Tyrrell-Ford. 14th in the championship with 5pts. **1990**: Lotus-Lamborghini test driver. Replaced the injured Martin Donnelly at the end of the year. No points. **1991**: Lotus-Judd in second half of the season. No points. **1992**: Lotus-Ford. 14th, 2pts. **1993**: Lotus-Ford. 9th, 14pts. **1994**: Lotus-Mugen, Ligier-Renault and Benetton-Ford. No points. **1995**: Benetton-Renault. 2 wins. 4th, 45pts. **1996**: Sauber-Ford. 14th. 4pts. **1997**: Sauber-Petronas. 10th, 15pts. **1998**: Sauber-Petronas. 15th, 1pt. **1999**: Stewart-Ford.

Number 17

Stewart - Ford
Johnny Herbert

If the Stewart SF-3 proves as competitive as it promises to be, Herbert could be catapulted back to the front of the field this season.

Here's the archetypal example of a driver who has been forced to construct his career according to the circumstances of the various teams he has known. With 129 starts he is one of the old brigade, and then some...Although he had a bright start with Benetton in 1989, things petered out quickly and it was not until 1992 that he got a full F1 programme together with Lotus. When he rejoined Benetton at the end of 1994 it looked like his big chance – but it was bad timing, as he had to be Michael Schumacher's team-mate.

Although it was difficult to shine in a team built around the German, he managed two wins when his partner was otherwise engaged in gravel traps. Keen to have a taste of life as a number one, he headed for Sauber and things went well – until Jean Alesi turned up. Almost from that moment, he was looking for another new home. And he was the ideal choice for Stewart, which needed an experienced driver who was aggressive, resilient, knew how

to win and could keep Barrichello on his guard. At this stage of his career, doubtless he might have wished for a more promising programme on paper, but such is fate. The Stewarts are both master diplomats, and they will do well to

maintain a harmonious relationship between their two drivers. Herbert and Barrichello are well aware that whichever of them gains the upper hand this year will have an easier job finding gainful future employment in F1.

PROST
Grand Prix

Alain Prost hung up his overalls for good to become a team owner. That said, away from the factory his experience is still a useful tool for Trulli and Panis.

It's up to the Prost-Peugeot AP02 to wipe away grim memories of last season's ineffective single-seater. There is real hunger for success at the team's Guyancourt HQ.

Peugeot A18
72-degree V10
Capacity: 2998cc
Length: 620mm
Width: 512mm
Height: 393mm
Weight: 120kg

Address:	Prost Grand Prix, Quartier des Sangliers, 7, avenue Eugène Freyssinet, 78280 Guyancourt, France
Tel:	00 33 (0) 1 39 30 11 00
Fax:	00 33 (0) 1 39 30 11 01
Internet:	www.peugeot.com/v10
Number of staff:	190
First GP:	Australia 1997
GP starts:	33
Points scored:	22 (average per GP: 0.66)
Best result in constructors' championship:	6th in 1997
Test driver:	Stéphane Sarrazin (France)
1998 record:	9th (1pt)

Managing director:
Alain Prost

Technical director:
Bernard Dudot

• **Plus points**
Technical, human and financial resources
 moving in the right direction
Extra support from Peugeot
Things can only get better

• **Minus points**
Suspect driver relationship
Engine is not of the latest generation
John Barnard's modus operandi

PEUGEOT
Prost GP

Prost AP02 – Tyres Bridgestone

The young Prost team has extra technical, human and financial resources to help it recover from its calamitous 1998 season.

Fresh technical regulations, a new engine, a revolutionary gearbox concept...with the benefit of hindsight it's easy to see that the size of the challenge facing the relatively new Prost team was somewhat daunting one year ago. Hence a calamitous campaign with the meagre consolation of a solitary point. All the same, the latter was enough to unify and inspire a team that has tripled in size in a few months: staffing levels have now risen to 190.

Difficult situations bring out the best in Alain Prost and he worked hard to make sure the latest car was ready early. Better still, he has secured the co-operation of his old ally John Barnard to add some design flair to the project. With Loïc Bigois in charge of aerodynamics and the quiet Briton looking after the mechanical side, Prost has put together a well-matched pair whose compatibility will be a great asset.

75

After a 1998 he wants to forget, this could be another fraught season for Olivier Panis. A victim of the limited competitiveness of last year's AP01, the Frenchman needs to prove that his fighting spirit is intact. But he comes into the new season in a brighter frame of mind – he has had some pins removed from his legs (a legacy of his 1997 accident in Canada) and is ready to reclaim a place among the front-runners.

There's no doubt that the new Prost AP02 is much better conceived than last year's model. But Olivier will need to remind himself of this to boost his morale after having to struggle at Melbourne with all the usual teething problems of a new car.

Date and place of birth:	2 September 1966, Lyon, France
Nationality:	French
Lives in:	Grenoble, France
Marital status:	married to Anne, two children
Height/Weight:	1.73m/74kg
Hobbies:	family, karting, cycling, jogging and gym work
Favourite food and drink:	pasta, Coca-Cola and water
First race:	Brazil 1994 (Ligier)
F1 statistics:	8th in 1995 (Ligier). 76 starts, 54 points, 1 win, 0 pole positions
F1 record:	**1994**: Ligier-Renault. 1 podium. 11th in the championship with 9pts. **1995**: Ligier-Mugen-Honda. 1 podium. 8th, 16pts. **1996**: Ligier-Mugen-Honda. 1 win. 9th, 13pts. **1997**: Prost-Mugen-Honda. 2 podiums. 10th, 16pts. **1998**: Prost-Peugeot. No points. **1999**: Prost-Peugeot.

Number 18

Prost - Peugeot

Olivier Panis

With an iron will and a good turn of speed, Olivier Panis is ready to get his career back on track after a brutal interruption at Montreal in 1997.

If 1999 is a key season for Prost GP in the medium term, it is even more so in the short term for Olivier Panis. He made solid, steady progress throughout a professional career highlighted by a magnificent victory in the 1996 Monaco GP. He looked set to build himself an even stronger reputation in 1997, when Alain Prost took over a team that had benefited from earlier investments by Flavio Briatore and Bruno Michel.

Things began brightly, but his hopes were ended abruptly by a dreadful accident during the Canadian GP. He suffered serious leg injuries but was fit to resume at the end of the year. Stronger and more determined than ever at the start of 1998, he was swiftly deflated by uncompetitive machinery. It was unreliable, not fast enough and it didn't suit his style of driving. His best efforts were destined to fail. Worse, his determination to redress the situation at any price led to

mistakes. It wasn't worth the risk and it was time for a rethink. Panis the Conqueror had become a shadow of his old self, a man concerned with building himself a bright new future. And that came in the form of a new, one-year contract – a means of putting

himself under pressure, to make sure he gave his all. The arrival of English designer John Barnard was one thing that kept him at Prost, and the team's determination to succeed was another. It's up to the AP02 to meet the challenge.

Young Jarno Trulli is widely tipped to be a bright star of the future. Highly rated by Alain Prost, he emerged with credit from a difficult 1998 season after coping calmly with stormy waters.

Although lost in the pack at Melbourne, the effervescent Jarno was able, nevertheless, to demonstrate the potential of the new Prost-Peugeot. If this potential is confirmed, the young Italian will have ample opportunity to display his own skills.

Date and place of birth:	13 July 1974, Pescara, Italy
Nationality:	Italian
Lives in:	Francavilla, Italy
Marital status:	single
Height/Weight:	1.73m/60kg
Hobbies:	model making, tennis, karting, mountain biking, jogging and swimming
Favourite food and drink:	pasta, pizza, admits to a weakness for chocolate, Coca-Cola
First race:	Australia 1997 (Minardi)
F1 statistics:	15th in 1997 (Minardi-Prost) and 1998 (Prost). 24 starts, 4 points, 0 wins, 0 pole positions
F1 record:	**1997**: Minardi-Ford until the Canadian GP. Prost-Mugen-Honda from France-Austria. 15th in the championship with 3pts. **1998**: Prost-Peugeot. 15th, 1pt. **1999**: Prost-Peugeot.

Number 19

Prost - Peugeot

Jarno Trulli

Pay heed to this charming young Italian – as soon as Prost finds its competitive edge, the world is going to notice.

This young Italian has several advantages over Olivier Panis. Working with what is, for him, a foreign team, he doesn't have to worry about national expectations or generate a family-type relationship. There is no need for him to get emotional when things aren't going so well and he isn't likely to be too concerned about the mood of those around him. He is also a naturally aggressive driver who can get something out of a less than perfect car – which is how Prost came by its only point in 1998. And the national media interest in Panis leaves him to work on his own in peace and quiet – which Olivier also manages to do, despite everything.

He also seems to have a little of the luck his French colleague is missing, such as in Australia at the start of the year, where he wasn't badly hindered by equipment that has still to be made reliable. He wasted the opportunity, however, trying too hard until the inevitable crash, which was a shame. Prost needs to play a delicate hand because there will be no lack of competition between the two drivers when the AP02 is working. Trulli has already complained that the team favours its other driver...who wants to make sure that John Barnard and his team don't strike up too much of a relationship with the Italian! Olivier Panis needs more than just a quick car this season, he needs a calm approach and strong moral support. If Trulli has a good season Prost will be the first to take up an option on his contract, but the French team should be under no illusions. Managed by Flavio Briatore, Jarno Trulli's future is probably not destined to be tied to Prost GP.

Technical director Gustav Brunner and aerodynamicist Jean-Claude Migeot have spared no expense building the M01, symbol of a new dawn at Minardi.

Abandoned by Esteban Tuero and his galaxy of Argentine backers, Minardi turned to Spain and the promising Marc Gené to put together a budget for 1999.

Address:	Minardi Team Spa,
	Via Spallanzani n°21,
	48018 Faenza (RA), Italy
Tel:	00 39 0546 620 480
Fax:	00 39 0546 620 998
Internet:	www.minardi.it
Number of staff:	120
First GP:	Brazil 1985
GP starts:	221
Points scored:	27 (average per GP: 0.12)
Best result in	
constructors' championship:	7th in 1991
Test driver:	Gaston Mazzacane (Argentina)
1998 record:	did not score

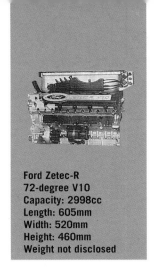

Ford Zetec-R
72-degree V10
Capacity: 2998cc
Length: 605mm
Width: 520mm
Height: 460mm
Weight not disclosed

Managing director:
Gabriele Rumi

Technical director:
Gustav Brunner

• **Plus points**
More ambitious than ever
Direct support from Ford
All-new car

• **Minus points**
Restricted means
Living in the shadow of Ferrari

FORD
Minardi

Minardi M01 – Tyres Bridgestone

The Faenza team is the last surviving example of a breed that, generally speaking, no longer exists in F1. It deserves its place in the big time, however, despite limited resources.

Gian Carlo Minardi might still be the symbolic figurehead of the lion-hearted Faenza team, but the prime mover in the business is Gabriele Rumi. A third generation member of an Italian industrial dynasty specialising in metallurgy and the preparation of alloys (background to the Fondmetal wheel company), he is also one of

the last – if not the last – of the genuine car enthusiasts in an F1 world where investment banks have an ever-greater influence. Today, as the team enters its 15th season, he hopes to reap the first real fruits from his obsession. Unlike last season, Gustav Brunner has been able to start afresh to create the new face of Faenza. The

MO1 chassis marks the beginning of a new Minardi generation. To complement a growing technical department, Rumi set out to appoint a heavyweight sporting director. He found one in Cesare Fiorio, late of Ferrari, Ligier, Forti and Prost. The bottom line, however, is that fierce pride is still hamstrung by a tight budget.

Marc Gené joins fellow rookies Pedro de la Rosa and Ricardo Zonta in F1. He has many things to learn. With a university degree to his name he is regarded as a bright young man – and he will need to focus every last drop of his intellect on motor sport.

Marc Gené will this year experience the excitement and fascination of driving an F1 car thanks to backing from a recently privatised Spanish telecommunications company. Such sponsorship is always useful to a team like Minardi.

Date and place of birth:	29 March 1974, Sabadell, Spain
Nationality:	Spanish
Lives in:	Bellaterra, Spain
Marital status:	single
Height/Weight:	1.73m/69kg
Hobbies:	deep-sea diving, reading, mountain biking, cinema and dance music
Favourite food and drink:	paella, milk
First race:	Australia 1999 (Minardi)
F1 record:	**1999**: Minardi-Ford. F1 rookie

Number 20

Minardi - Ford
Marc Gené

A difficult start for the Spaniard who had to retire in Australia after a coming-together with Jarno Trulli.

In all honesty, Marc Gené would have wagered a lifetime's supply of paella against anyone who forecast that he would be racing in F1 this year. And he would have been totally confident of winning the bet. He was invited to test a Minardi as part of his prize for winning last year's new Open Fortuna by Nissan series. He did 30 laps, shook the team boss's hand, smiled for the Spanish media and went home. One month later he was called up for a proper seat fitting and to cover enough laps at Barcelona to earn himself an F1 superlicence.

It was a fairy story that came true partly because of his ability, and partly because of a favourable mix of other circumstances. Such as, for instance, the disappearance of young Argentine Esteban Tuero, who was reported to have lost his appetite for F1 after a crash in Japan last season. And there was the hard work done by Marc's elder brother Jordi, himself a racer of repute, and his manager Adrian Campos, an ex-Minardi driver. And there was the Spanish telecom company that wanted to follow the lead of Repsol, which had backed Pedro de la Rosa's F1 graduation, by going on a global media offensive of its own. With a wise head on his shoulders, Gené knows his lack of experience will make it hard for him to race at the same level as his compatriot. The business management graduate understands that patience is the key, and won't feel let down if the team focuses its effort on Badoer to begin with.

Quick and smart, Luca Badoer appreciates a chance to return to the team he drove for in 1995. An F1 rookie in 1993 and Ferrari test driver since 1998, he has been loaned to Gian Carlo Minardi's team for the season.

Minardi is relying on Badoer's experience to develop the M01. More than that, it hopes to score a clutch of points with the Italian, who is pleased to have a chance to race once more.

Date and place of birth:	25 January 1971, Montebelluna (Treviso), Italy
Nationality:	Italian
Lives in:	Monte Carlo
Marital status:	single
Height/Weight:	1.70m/58kg
Hobbies:	snowmobiling and Italian music
Favourite food and drink:	grilled meat, orange juice
First race:	South Africa 1993 (BMS Lola-Ferrari)
F1 statistics:	Never classified. 34 starts, 0 points, 0 wins, 0 pole positions
F1 record:	**1993**: BMS Scuderia Italia Lola-Ferrari. **1994**: Minardi-Ford, test driver. **1995**: Minardi-Ford. **1996**: Forti-Ford. **1998-present**: Ferrari test driver. **1999**: Minardi-Ford.

Number 21

Minardi - Ford
Luca Badoer

To the Italian's great disappointment, the new M01 did not get off to a flying start in Melbourne.

Moving forward one small step at a time, Luca Badoer finally landed at Ferrari – albeit only as test driver. It's a well-paid job, of course, and he has even earned the respect of the Italian media for the work he does on behalf of the two race drivers, notably Schumacher. But it's frustrating for a man who won the 1992 F3000 title, and who was once regarded as the brightest prospect in Italian racing. And how annoying for a driver with such a combination of pace and technical prowess that he can only demonstrate as much behind closed doors. And that's why Gian Carlo Minardi and Gabriele Rumi approached Ferrari directors Luca di Montezemolo and Jean Todt (they are all on good terms again now, having buried the hatchet after Minardi wooed designer Gustav Brunner away from Ferrari).

The affirmative response came quickly, but the deal took time to sort out because Badoer wanted, quite rightly, a salary to match his

solid reputation. And he didn't bring any sponsorship with him – not even so much as a packet of cigarettes, of which Ferrari has no shortage. Eventually it was all worked out and Minardi has a driver capable of getting the best

from the new M01/99. Ferrari test work remains his main job, but that's a minor handicap – and one Minardi can live with. It's now up to Badoer to get back into the swing of F1 and to deal with the hazards of racing in the pack.

85

Following an FIA ruling, the dual liveries of Lucky Strike (Villeneuve) and 555 (Zonta) have been merged into one. By the time it made its F1 debut, the new BAR team had already felt the full force of authority.

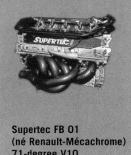

Supertec FB 01
(né Renault-Mécachrome)
71-degree V10
Capacity not disclosed
Length: 623mm
Width: 542mm
Height: 395mm
Weight: 120kg

Address:

British American Racing,
Brackley, Northamptonshire
NN13 7BD, England

Tel: (44) 0128 084 0402
Fax: (44) 0128 084 0403
Internet: www.britishamericanracing.com
Number of staff: 220
First GP: Australia 1999
Test driver: Patrick Lemarié (France)

Managing director:
Craig Pollock

Technical director:
Adrian Reynard

- **Plus points**

Great resources – both human and financial
Strength of Reynard as a technical partner
Two top-line drivers
High-profile image

- **Minus points**

Target of envy because of the above
Short of collective experience
Fractious relationship (already) with the F1 authorities

BAR B SUPERTEC
British American Racing

BAR PR 01 – Tyres Bridgestone

BRITISH AMERICAN RACING

With the powerful support of British American Tobacco, the strength of Reynard's technical department and the signing of Jacques Villeneuve, Craig Pollock's team has already established itself as one of the year's big talking points.

In December 1997, Craig Pollock, Adrian Reynard and Martin Broughton of British American Tobacco announced they had completed the purchase of Tyrrell, which would be absorbed into the new British American Racing organisation. It signalled the birth of BAR and the disappearance of one of Formula One's most famous names. While Tyrrell endured a quiet final F1 season in 1998, BAR's adopted home in Brackley was already a hive of activity. Chassis designer Reynard was preparing to move into an ultra-modern new facility where its own staff of 280 would work alongside the 220 personnel of British American Racing.

That's where Malcolm Oastler set to work. As chief designer, it was his heavy responsibility to produce a car for 1997 champion Jacques Villeneuve. On 7 March, the Canadian joined Pollock, Reynard and Broughton in witnessing the realisation of a project which had first been discussed during the build-up to his Indianapolis 500 victory in 1995: the launch of a team that could challenge for the F1 title.

For Jacques Villeneuve the risk of the gamble is outweighed by the excitement of the challenge. He has the opportunity to be right at the heart of a brand-new F1 team. With the help of his long-time manager Craig Pollock and single-seater wizard Adrian Reynard, the no-nonsense Canadian wants to demonstrate that BAR is a force to be reckoned with.

After a politically-charged off-season – especially as far as BAR's dual livery plan was concerned – Jacques Villeneuve was raring to get stuck into his race programme and notch up a few decent results in a car that appears to be competitive.

Date and place of birth:	9 April 1971, St Jean-sur-Richelieu, Quebec
Nationality:	Canadian
Lives in:	Monte Carlo
Marital status:	single
Height/Weight:	1.68m/67kg
Hobbies:	alpine skiing, roller blading, reading, computer games and playing guitar
Favourite food and drink:	pasta, milk
First race:	Australia 1996 (Williams)
F1 statistics:	World champion in 1997 (Williams). 50 starts, 188 points, 11 wins, 13 pole positions.
F1 record:	**1996**: Williams-Renault. 4 wins, 3 poles, 2nd in the championship with 76pts. **1997**: Williams-Renault. 7 wins, 10 poles. World champion, 81pts. **1998**: Williams-Mécachrome. 5th, 21pts. **1999**: BAR-Supertec.

Number

British American Racing
Jacques
Villeneuve

Is Jacques Villeneuve really so different to his famous father? His capacity for reflection, analytical tendencies and appreciation of the limit come more from his mother's side. From his dad, he has inherited a taste for speed on the ground, on snow, sea or in the air. He has his father's mild anti-conformist streak, and occasionally provocative manner. In essence, he just wants to live life on his own terms without worrying what anyone else thinks. He wants to be comfortable with his lot.

For all that he sometimes appears slightly disinterested, Villeneuve has great strength of character and spirit. He decided late on to become a racing driver, without having any karting experience. And given that he was the son of you-know-who, that took a great deal of resolve. It wasn't long before he showed his willingness to adapt by abandoning his friends and comfortable home life in Europe for a spell of exile in Japan. And then

he showed more bottle by springing from almost nowhere to race in America's premier Indycar series. Everything went incredibly well and he acquired such a strong reputation that Bernie Ecclestone did absolutely everything within his power to link the powerful Villeneuve name with F1. And he arrived with style, picking up wins and, in his second year, the world title. The most impressive thing he has done, however, is to make a name for himself, in the same way

Damon Hill has done. Except that Jacques has perhaps done it to even greater effect, because Damon's current generation of supporters is unlikely to have been enthusiastic about his father. Having achieved what he set out to do, Jacques has now targeted a fresh challenge – an equal source of motivation and fun. He is driving for a team built up around him, among friends. Perhaps it won't make him world champion again, but he'll be enjoying himself.

The Australian GP showed that BAR still has some work to do. Villeneuve retired because of rear wing failure.

89

Ricardo Zonta is considered a particularly talented newcomer. His career has been astutely managed so far and he enters F1 in a promising situation. BAR was a wise choice – and it's up to him to showcase his talent.

After his F1 race baptism, Ricardo Zonta and his team need to pick up invaluable experience – and quickly – if they are to obtain strong results this year.

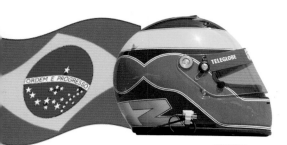

Date and place of birth:	23 March 1976, Curitiba, Brazil
Nationality:	Brazilian
Lives in:	Monte Carlo
Marital status:	single
Height/Weight:	1.72m/64kg
Hobbies:	water sports and music – particularly Australian and Brazilian
First race:	Australia 1999 (BAR)
F1 record:	**1999**: BAR-Supertec. F1 rookie

Number

23

British American Racing

Ricardo Zonta

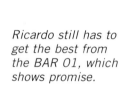

Ricardo still has to get the best from the BAR 01, which shows promise.

"In the Seventies and Eighties Brazil was a rich seam of F1 greats," says Ricardo. "Fittipaldi, Piquet, Ayrton Senna...Me? By the time I was ten I had already made my mind up that I was going to be a famous driver. And that's when my career started, when my dad bought me a kart." Just ten years later he was winning F3000 races, and the following season Jordan gave him his first F1 break during a five-day test at Silverstone.

During his stint he posted a best time of 1m 31.09s while Mika Hakkinen managed 1m 30.33s in a McLaren development chassis. It was proof once again that Eddie Jordan knew a good thing when he saw it, but this time it was Mercedes who pounced. Zonta was given a multi-year contract that started with two roles: McLaren F1 tester and frontline GT racer for Mercedes. As he racked up a sequence of pole positions and race victories he added the 1998 GT title to the F3000 crown he had won the previous season.

"I could have moved into F1 a couple of years earlier," he says, "but I wanted to wait for the best opportunity. Working with AMG and Mercedes was a great experience and it gave me race and technical experience that almost matched F1 standards." If biding your time means hanging around for a McLaren-Mercedes deal then it has to be worth it. But McLaren was full for 1999 with Hakkinen and Coulthard, and he had been promised an F1 deal, so it was time to negotiate. The upshot was a place with the fledgling BAR-Supertec outfit – and there could be no finer place to start. He has the best possible team and team-mate to guide him into F1, but Craig Pollock and Jacques Villeneuve won't want to give away too much. Anything he learns this year could come back to haunt them one day in the future, as and when Zonta signs for McLaren.

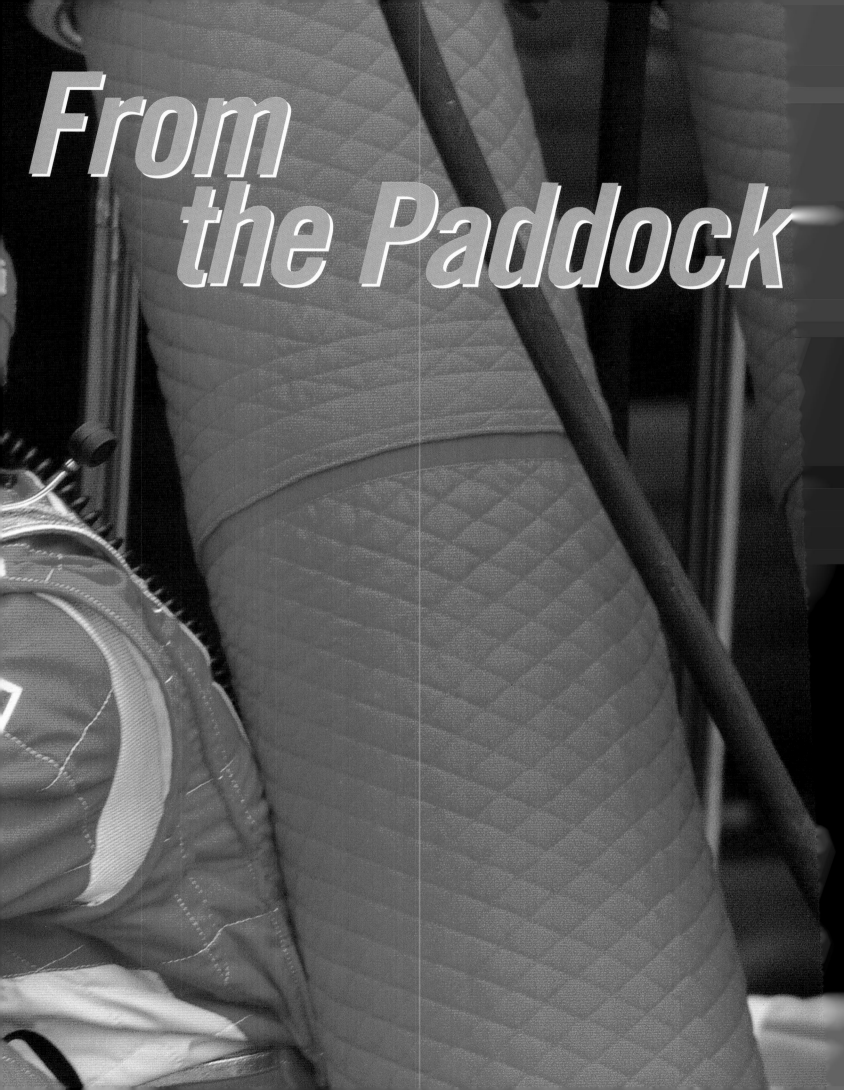

From the Paddock

After three years of hard work, Michael Schumacher wants to reap the rewards of his endeavours. This accomplished sportsman will spare no effort in his bid to get the better of the Silver Arrows.

The brand-new F399 and Jody Scheckter's title-winning 312 T4 are separated by a 20-year drought that has done little to diminish the Scuderia's popularity.

Ferrari: The need to win

Words are no longer enough

It's the 20th anniversary of Ferrari's last world drivers' title – and even the most patient tifosi have had enough of waiting. Other fans than these would have lost interest long ago. And now that all F1 teams are fitted with the same tyres, the Scuderia has lost the only thing that made it obviously different – for better or worse – to its main rival. The circumstances are now right for a duel on equal terms. For Ferrari, it's now or never.

A 20-year gulf separates Jody Scheckter's title-winning Ferrari 312 T4 and the brand-new F399 chassis – two fallow decades from which the Scuderia's popularity has somehow emerged intact. It's proof positive that motor racing can be an affair of the heart, not the mind, but the magic does have its limits. There will come a point when it no longer works for those who support the team technically and financially.

"I hope that 1999 won't be the season when I have to put my objectives on hold for yet another year," said Gianni Agnelli as he left Fiorano shortly after the launch of the F399. Honorary president of the Fiat Group, a mythical figure who will one day be regarded as a kind of demi-god (just as Enzo Ferrari was after his death), Agnelli doesn't say much – but his words ring loud and true. As for his latest observation, there is no doubt that it will strike fear into Ferrari president Luca di Montezemolo for some time.

Over the years, Ferrari has tried to maintain a certain status that sets it apart from rival teams. It has tackled English know-how with a blend of pride and Latin flair. But that approach has to change. Patience and obsession have their limits. Henceforth it must no longer be a case of waiting for a

committed to that path in order to respect its tradition and preserve its culture. Besides, it has the financial and technical means to meet the challenge.

That said, in some respects Ferrari is a team like any other. Having previously wooed the best driver and the finest technical

It was a glorious start to the season for Jean Todt's men – though their winning car was not the one they expected.

rival to break down in order to thrive. It's time to start winning on a regular basis. True, the Ferrari route – building its own chassis and engine – is not the most straight-forward, but the team is

brains from Benetton, it has now pinched one of its sponsors (FedEx), too. That shows that it intends to fight on the same terms and use the same tactics as everyone else.

What Ferrari has lost of its Latin spirit under the Todt regime, it has made up with calmness and efficiency. A change of approach was necessary, because sharp pit work can sometimes have the biggest influence on the outcome of a grand prix.

"The directors of Fiat have not put any more pressure on us this year than they have in the past," stresses di Montezemolo. "They still have absolute faith and respect for the work we have done in the past few seasons to reach our current level of competitiveness. I just hope we can reward their interest and enthusiasm with some hard results.

"Last year, when the F300 was launched, I never promised a world title. I simply said that we would be capable of winning more races and competing for the championship. And that's what we did right up to the final race of the season. The only disappointment was that the title slipped from our grasp at the very last moment, for the second successive season. I have now asked everyone to make sure we don't go through the same unhappy experience again."

A simple objective

The objective is simple: in order to make sure no more titles are lost at the end of the campaign, Ferrari has to be in a position to win races from the off. And for that reason di Montezemolo has refused to utter even the slightest word about winning championships. This time, he wants to make sure the team can walk before it tries to run.

"We are through with never-ending promises," he says. "They can be broken because of a grain of sand in the engine or a bizarre on-track incident, the kind of thing over which we have no control. But that hasn't stopped us fixing clear targets, which is to do better than we did in 1998. It's a logical ambition, but just because we were second last season it doesn't follow that we will only accept being first this time. Doing better means getting off to a quicker start this time.

"And if we are going to improve on track, we have to do likewise in all domains – in the research department, in the wind tunnel, in the assembly shop, in the pits. I don't want to add anything else because words don't help. The only thing I have promised my men, and which I will promise to you, is that we will be relentless in our quest to win the battle. Every member of this team is willing and determined. We must start and finish the season brightly – and rest assured that we will do our best."

Sporting director Jean Todt dismisses the notion of any bluster. "There is no more point saying we are going to win the title this year than there was last year or there will be next year," he says. "But for a team like this the championship has to be our objective, and we have the means to enable us to do it. All I can say is that we intend to fight even harder this season than we have done in the past."

The two Ferrari bosses have a point. 1998 was by no means a bad season – and in terms of points scored it was the best in Ferrari's history. In the end they just fell slightly short – and the points they lost in the Spa crash between Schumacher and Coulthard might have tipped the balance. By such twists of fate can the pressure to succeed be heightened.

It affects those who prepare the cars as much as it does the drivers, who have to absorb incredible mental strain during the course of a race weekend. A few minutes to set the fastest possible qualifying lap, a few seconds to make the best start...and concentration has to be absolute every second of the way to minimise the chances of a mistake, and to ensure the best race strategy. There's no point trying to work out what that adds up to over a season of 17 races. In short, it's a tough job.

This season, the Scuderia's mission is clear: to be competitive from the moment the teams hit Australia. And it has a number of key assets to strengthen its hand, not least a strong, organised and balanced technical team that works well together – and the F399 is its second car. The driver line-up is the same for the fourth straight season. There is absolutely nothing they and the team don't know about each other. And now they have the same tyres as everyone else, too, a factor that Todt believes cost them dear in 1998.

"The war between Bridgestone and Goodyear was unsettling for us," he says. "Our American supplier had to give second best to Bridgestone in the first six races, and that was a big handicap. We made up ground later on, but the consequences of our poor results at the start of the year were ultimately too much to overcome. I'm sure that if we had taken a step forward two or three races earlier, the outcome of the title would have

Despite its winning start, Ferrari didn't return from Australia with great peace of mind. Although McLaren remains the main threat, Jordan showed signs of a potential challenge, too.

been different. Now we are back to a traditional contest between driver, chassis and engine, there might be some pleasant surprises in store for us in 1999. Come what may, we have no further need to make any excuses about tyres."

But won't Ferrari lose out because McLaren has a year's experience with Bridgestone? Technical director Ross Brawn dismisses such talk. "Perhaps at the very beginning," he says, "but only because McLaren already knows exactly how these tyres work and how the Japanese manufacturer works, but that advantage won't last."

The F399

That might partially explain the speed differential between McLaren and Ferrari during this season's first grand prix in Australia, but ultimately the Anglo-German racers ran into huge reliability problems. And although Eddie Irvine won for Ferrari, Schumacher stumbled and missed out on a chance to get a flying 10-point start while his main rivals were drawing a blank. Technically, the F399 has nothing to be ashamed about. It is now 20kg heavier and features an innovative electronic power steering system. It doesn't give much of an advantage during a single lap, but its benefits are said to be considerable over a race distance. Although the system

adds 5kg to the weight, it gives the drivers greater consistency, better feedback and more comfort, as the weight of the steering is speed sensitive. The F399 has several other new features. The suspension components are now all carbon and the rear spring-damper units are now located vertically on either side of the gearbox.

The 048 engine is closely related to the old 047, but has several key advantages. The centre of gravity is lower by 5mm, it's 5-6kg lighter, has a broader spread of usable power and operates more efficiently at higher temperatures. The cooling system has thus been made slightly smaller, so the sidepods are a little lower and that enables the car to cut through the air more efficiently. And that's how you claw back some of the straight line speed that was missing in the F300. But will this be enough to create the Ferrari the tifosi – and Schumacher – have been craving?

"On paper," says Jean Todt, "we appear to have moved on from the F300 if we listen to what our aerodynamic and engine specialists say, and if we add up all the new figures. If you asked me to sum up the F399 in a couple of words I'd say it is well finished and very complete. It is the first time since I have been with Ferrari that I have seen the guys from the engine, chassis and aerodynamic

departments working so closely together. But as always I won't trust anything until I see the evidence of our work on the track. After the general hullabaloo at Melbourne you don't learn a great deal in Brazil, because that circuit is not like any other. The San Marino Grand Prix, race three, will be the first chance to have some

Eddie Irvine's role could become even more important this season than it was in the past.

idea what the 1999 season really holds for Ferrari."

Even so, in an ideal world the team would be leading the world championship by the time its first home race of the year comes around...and if that's the case at least part of di Montezemolo's wishes will have been fulfilled.

MASS
JONES
PIRONI
FITTIPALDI
JABOUILLE
ANDRETTI
LAMMERS
WATSON
PIQUET
JARIER
SCHECKTER

Twenty years on,
Jody
Scheckter looks back...

Back in the spotlight through force of circumstance, Ferrari's last world champion looks back on his 1979 season...

From high up in his Victorian house in Onslow Gardens, in the heart of London's fashionable Kensington, the former world champion turned successful businessman savours a certain irony in the current level of interest his 1979 world title attracts. Surprised by his involuntary media comeback, Scheckter is nonetheless careful to make the most of it and doesn't need asking twice to open the door to his personal recollections.

"At the end of the Seventies simply being a Ferrari driver was almost as good as winning the world title," he says, "so to do both...well, you can imagine. It really was a fantastic campaign for me, a year blessed by the gods. I won in Monaco and in front of the tifosi at Monza, I picked up the world championship...I was very, very fortunate. Throughout the whole of 1979 absolutely nothing went wrong, even though things didn't climax until fairly late on. But you had to be careful, because the more the pressure built up, the better you had to be to handle it. From that aspect, 1979 certainly wasn't an easy year."

But surely, we asked him, he must have been affected by the unexpected drawback in the third race of the year, on home soil at Kyalami, South Africa?

"It wasn't a problem," he says,

instantly. "Let's just say it put a little more pressure on my shoulders. I was supposed to be number one and the fact that my team-mate Gilles Villeneuve had beaten me in successive races, at Long Beach and Kyalami, put me in a delicate position. But although he'd beaten me fair and square in America, his win in South Africa was a product of circumstance because I had tyre trouble. I know many people think Gilles was simply there to back me up in 1979, but that was never the case.

The only instruction we had was to hold our positions if we were running alone at the head of the field and there was no longer any threat from elsewhere."

When he talks about Villeneuve, his voice lowers and the atmosphere is charged with palpable emotion. Throughout 1979 he and the late French-Canadian became great friends – and he doesn't want to forget that.

"We had complete trust in each other and that was the basis of our friendship," he says. "The whole

The Ferrari 312 T4 was Mauro Forghieri's work of genius – and it hasn't been forgotten. What will people say about the F399 20 years from now?

Jody Scheckter: age has not withered his 1979 championship success!

99

1979 could not have been better for Jody. Not only did he win Monaco on his way to the crown, he also won the Italian GP in front of the delirious tifosi.

In Scheckter's title season the Ligiers of Laffite and Depailler were among Ferrari's toughest rivals. Who remembers that nowadays?

world tended to think of him as a carefree driver, perhaps even a bit of a crackpot. But that wasn't the case at all, even if he enjoyed playing up to that image. Contrary to what was said about him, the risks he took were absolutely measured and he was a dedicated professional. The first time he took me from Monaco to Modena in his car, I was very nervous because he had this reputation for being a bit of a nutcase. In fact, although he drove very quickly, he was very smooth, very confident and he didn't start acting like a madman until we got to Modena...He liked to maintain his reputation. It

amused him and he liked to hear people saying things like, 'Here comes that lunatic Villeneuve.'

"And he was the same during a grand prix weekend, he preferred to be man of the lap rather than man of the race. In all honesty I think that's why I won the title and not him. His thing was to rip through sets of tyres in order to set a qualifying time rather than trying to work out a good race set-up..."

To interrupt his affectionate but grief-tinged reveries, we asked him about that year's winning car, the Ferrari 312 T4.

"It was a car that was easy to understand straight out of the box," he says, "despite the fact that the Michelin tyres of the day were sometimes inconsistent. That said, the tyres were a minor problem compared to those caused by the shape of the T4's flat-12 engine. At that time airflow beneath the chassis had a tremendous influence on its handling and Mauro Forghieri, our designer and technical director, didn't want to believe that we might have reached, or indeed gone beyond, our car's development limits. With each successive race the T4 became more and more edgy to drive and eventually we passed the critical threshold. We pleaded with Mauro to tidy up the floorpan, but he

turned a deaf ear until Enzo Ferrari called a meeting in Maranello one Monday morning. After railing about how the team was being run – which was also relevant – he demanded that changes were made and then listened to our recommendations. Gilles and I were in total agrement on every point and we asked for this, that and the other to be modified. We told him that any gains might be small, but there were things worth trying in that direction. The commendatore listened attentively ...and approved. Without those changes, there would never have been a world title on my CV."

Jody Scheckter had a meteoric rise in motor sport, but one year after he was crowned he quit the sport and went off to make his fortune in America. Twenty years later, back in Europe to watch over his sons, history has caught up with him.

And today, 20 years later, that championship success continues to influence his life.

"It's funny," he says, "but it feels like it has taken all this time for people to realise I was ever world champion. I gave up my racing career one year later and headed pretty quickly for America. I didn't make a great deal of fuss about my decision and it was a clean break. In the States F1 racing is barely known and it's perfectly true that I never really revelled in my title of world champion. But I'm making the most of it now. Life has striking surprises in store sometimes and," he says, smiling, "I suppose I ought to thank Ferrari for not winning the title since."

But he does not think his status as Ferrari's most recent champion will last for long.

"Looking at the last two seasons there is no doubt that the Scuderia is on the right track," he says. "In terms of technical and human resources, President di Montezemolo has invested in everything Ferrari needs to be successful. It's taken a few years, sure, but there is no question that the team has now got what it needs. Ferrari was only beaten last season because McLaren had managed to get absolutely every last detail just so. In one sense, Ferrari was actually a little unlucky last year. The technical team built up around Michael Schumacher looks the part and they are all working together very constructively. If you add the fact that everyone is running the same tyres this year, I think you'll find Ferrari is in good shape to win the title this year. And I think they should do it…"

The life and works of Jody Scheckter

Born on 29 January 1950 in East London, South Africa, Jody Scheckter shot like a meteor through motor racing's constellation. His first few Formula One races were striking, in every sense of the word – remember the spectacular multiple pile-up he caused in the opening stages of the 1973 British GP? Yet in 1974, his first full season, he was in contention for the title.

It would be another five years, however, before "Baby Bear" (a nickname borne of his hairstyle and sometimes clumsy manner) was crowned. Within a year of his crowning glory he was off to the United States to build up a successful career as a manufacturer of military training equipment used by the police and American armed forces. Having returned to Europe two years ago, he now oversees the racing careers of his two sons, Toby and Tomas.

1970: South African racing champion with a Renault 8 Gordini.
1971: Came to England to race in Formula Ford.
1972: European F2 Championship with McLaren; F1 debut with McLaren in America.
1973: Five grands prix with McLaren.
1974: Two F1 wins for Tyrrell, third in the championship.
1975: Stayed with Tyrrell; seventh in the world championship (one win).
1977: Switched to Wolf. Second in the championship with three wins.
1978: Still with Wolf, but no wins and only classified seventh.
1979: Moved to Ferrari. Won three races and the championship title.
1980: Only 19th in the rankings after a dismal year for Ferrari. Retired from the sport at the end of the year.

Jean Alesi A doyen still raring to go

Alesi's stunning grand prix debut for Tyrrell remains fresh in the memory.

Alesi's stunning grand prix debut for Tyrrell remains fresh in the memory.

When he hung up his crash helmet, Gerhard Berger transferred to his pal Jean Alesi the honour of being Formula One's doyen. With 151 races under his belt, the Avignon racer has developed a philosophical outlook on a sport which has always been – and will long remain – his passion.

Last winter we could see you were a man refreshed because you had lost six kilos. Anything new to report this time?
No, nothing special. I have to say that last year's diet was more a psychological goal than a physical necessity. I had lost my motivation at Benetton and I wasn't training as hard as usual.

It got to the stage where I wanted to lose weight not just to improve my physique, but to give myself a psychological boost, to make myself feel a bit fresher.

After 11 seasons in F1, how do you spend the off-season? Do you switch off completely or are you always on the phone to the factory to find out how your new car is coming along?
When I first started I was aware that Ayrton Senna used to spend two months in Brazil and cut himself off completely from the sport to which he was totally devoted. But I don't think you can do that nowadays. There's a very short period of free time between the end of the season and the start of testing – and you can't get away without taking part in the tests. I switch off for about three weeks,

but that's it. After Japan I devote myself entirely, but briefly, to my family.

It's your second year with Sauber and I'm sure Diniz would agree that you are the number one driver. You have got a good budget and a good Ferrari engine. What are your realistic expectations?
In 11 years of F1 I have learned lots of things – including the art of how to be realistic about things. Whenever a new car is launched, who hasn't said that they envisaged

world titles, race wins, podium finishes or regular top six results? Who hasn't predicted that their new car would be capable of qualifying in the top ten? If you mix champagne and promises a

sponsor will he happy and part of their investment will already have been justified. But after all the bright predictions, you have to get stuck into testing – and then the first grand prix. That's when things really take shape, that's reality and that never changes. It might evolve a little, but it never changes.

Jean gave his all for the Ferrari marque he loves – but he got precious few results by way of return.

McLaren and Ferrari will still be what they have been in the past, but Williams has faded a bit since Adrian Newey's departure and I don't see them getting back to the top this season.

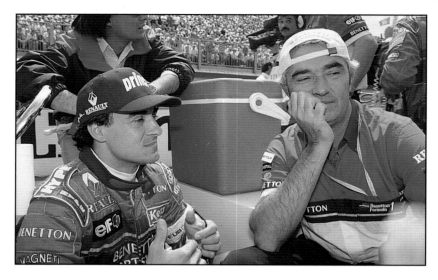

We've had four world champions in as many seasons. Is that variety a sign that the machinery now definitely plays a greater role than the driver?
Of course! We've had the Williams-Renault years, now perhaps we are entering a McLaren-Mercedes era. It's also worth noting that we have entered a new generation, after the death of Senna and the retirements of the old guard, such as Mansell, Prost and Piquet.

With a top-class car at his disposal, Schumacher was in a league of his own. Now we have to look at the seasonal fluctuations in the state of equipment – Hill and Villeneuve benefited from the strength of Williams, as perhaps did Hakkinen at the start of McLaren's resurgence.

There isn't really a driver who can establish himself as the best of a generation on the basis of his talent alone. The competitiveness of the car is vital, even if things appear to have levelled out a bit. I even wonder whether the various cycles don't depend more on technical directors, such as John Barnard and Adrian Newey. You know, one day they find an edge

because they have a great engine to work with or a huge research and development budget. It's a circumstantial thing where everything comes together in the right place at the right time. And if a driver is worth his salt, he'll turn such a situation to his advantage.

If you haven't got a McLaren or a Ferrari, do you ever get the impression you are racing in a kind of second division?
All I can say is that the huge financial advantage those two teams have does not produce an enormous performance advantage. Sure, they are the dominant forces – but the others aren't left completely for dead, even though they have only a half or a third of the budget. When I started out at Tyrrell, after 40 or 50 laps it was normal for the dominant teams of the day to put you a full lap behind. The sport still has its major powers, but things are now much closer in the following pack

What has been the biggest single change during your 11 years of F1?
The safety advances we have made have been quite extraordinary – with both the circuits and the cars. I suppose we don't think about it much because it's a part of our daily routine, but we set off on a qualifying lap or from the starting grid without the slightest apprehension. You think about the possibility of a collision, the chances of going off the track, a spin or a mechanical failure, but you don't worry about it. It's when

It was close friend Gerhard Berger who steered Alesi towards Sauber at the end of the 1997 season.

Alesi came to Benetton at the wrong time and suffered dearly for the team's loss of Ross Brawn and Rory Byrne to Ferrari. Given the state of technical freefall, it didn't take long before the drivers were getting the blame...

you are testing sometimes at a circuit that doesn't meet F1 criteria that you realise how much progress has been made. You see places where the barriers are too low, the debris fencing is all over the place, there are no gravel traps and the escape roads are too short ... If you go to a track from which F1 has been absent for 10 years, you'll soon notice the difference.

It's the same with the cars. Whenever I see a car from five or six seasons ago I ask myself whether we must have been completely insane to take the kind of risks we did. It makes you appreciate the difference.

The ability of race officials, track marshals, scrutineers and race directors has also come on. It's no longer a case that he who shouts loudest gets his own way.

How do you feel about the media explosion, the demands of the teams' marketing departments, the requirements of personal sponsors and the partners of the big teams?
Progress has been striking in this area, too! I have gone along with it without suffering. It's a fact of modern F1 life. An hour before the start, when we should be trying to shut ourselves off to get focused for the race, we have to join our VIP guests in the Paddock Club to talk them through each corner, explain how to change gear and discuss every function of the steering wheel and dashboard. And then there's

the autograph session. You can't escape – and it's just part of the price you have to pay for the sport's popularity. Everything has been professionalised to an incredible level. Even the press! The gutter journalists have slipped away; an elite has been established and has stayed put to work intelligently within the various different areas of F1. It has to be said that everything is now organised and orchestrated to the minute and no team makes do without staff to handle marketing, promotion, press and PR. The FIA has also played its part with conferences organised to take part at set times on certain days.

Is it harder to get into F1 now than it used to be?
It's just as hard as ever. Not only do you have to catch the boss's eye, but also you have to be lucky enough to join the right team at the right time. The problem has always been there and it won't ever go away. That said, young drivers tend to be a lot better prepared nowadays than they were in my day. I started in Formula One without any testing and, physically speaking, I was ill prepared. And I wasn't much better technically. It felt as though I'd landed on another planet. Today, many rookies are lucky enough to have been a test driver, or to have worked in a category where the technology and methods of working are almost the same as they are in

F1. They know the finer points of technical discussion and they understand what an engineer expects of them.

Do you feel sad that, in the modern era, the public see grand prix drivers taking part only in F1? In the old days you saw them at Le Mans, in F2, even in rallies and hillclimbs.
It would be as much fun for the driver as it would for the public, I promise you! But it's just not

Hurt by his disappointing time with Benetton, Jean found refuge in the family atmosphere at Sauber. And the love story continues to this day ...

possible for a number of reasons. There are 17 grands prix per season, plus so many test sessions and a clutch of promotional duties during the off-season. And you have to remember that virtually all

Peter Sauber and Jean Alesi have absolute faith in each other. The boss is counting on the Frenchman's great experience to lead his team forward to better things.

Loyalty has been a strong feature of Alesi's career – and he's never far from reminding you of his strong attachment to Ferrari.

F1 drivers are tied to major sponsors – whether car manufacturers or tobacco companies – who are anxious to retain their services on an exclusive basis. There's also the question of unnecessary extra risk – drivers are very heavily insured by their teams, and are asked not to chance their arm too often.

F1 has also lost some of its traditional artisan teams...

It's a question of efficiency over romance. Alain Prost has taken over from Guy Ligier; Craig Pollock has done likewise to Ken Tyrrell. That's how the world moves on, but I was shocked at the way Ken was shoved aside in the BAR/Tyrrell takeover. It showed a total lack of respect for one of F1's great characters. We still have two enthusiasts in Gabriele Rumi and Gian Carlo Minardi – but for how long. F1 needs major manufacturers: Honda, Ferrari, BMW, Renault, Audi, Toyota, Mercedes, General Motors, Peugeot, Aston Martin, Jaguar, Alfa-Romeo, Ford... those are the names we ought to see in F1!

D'you ever regret that you haven't savoured the joy of having a good car at the right time, unlike Hill, Villeneuve, Schumacher or Hakkinen?

No. I will end my career without a CV to match theirs, but I think I'll have been through a rich seam of emotions unknown to any of them. We all take what we want from F1: of course they are happy with their lot, but so am I with mine. I wouldn't want to change any aspect of my career. No one, not a single race – apart from what sadly happened at San Marino in 1994.

Does a 35-year-old still drive like a 25-year-old?

No. Your driving is smoother, you think more about your track moves and the technical side. By definition youth signifies a lack of experience, so you are always curious, always feeling your way, you don't have a particular game plan. At 35 you appreciate your own limits – and those of the car. You are better able to handle situations that, 10 years earlier, might have left you panicking and rattled.

Given your experience, d'you think you have a role to play for young drivers?

Yes and no. The fact I have age and experience on my side does not give me licence to lecture a young driver about how he should or should not behave. Each to his own. On the other hand, the way I conduct myself on the track, in the paddock, during pre-race briefings or meetings between drivers could be useful. You try to set a good example, and above all to be a sportsman.

Why are you so interested in the Grand Prix Drivers' Association?

The GPDA is the best thing we could have. It's not a state within a state, but a group of drivers who speak openly about subjects that are dear to them. Everyone comes face to face with those who have played a trick on them, hit them at the start of a race or refused to let them pass even when blue flags are waved. And they have a chance to explain themselves. Dialogue is a great thing because it brings stuff out in the open and allows people to get major grievances off their chest. I'm sure that if we had something like this in the past we would never have known about the bitter rivalries between Mansell and Piquet, Mansell and Prost or Prost and Senna.

His win in Canada 1995 has been the only one to date.

Kumiko: an attentive companion.

This season Alesi's main objective is to give his Swiss team its first F1 win ... and perhaps to move on to a better drive in 2000. Whatever happens, he is not about to step down from grand prix racing ...

Idol of British motor racing fans, Damon Hill has found in Jordan a team capable of getting him back to the front of the field. Boosted by extra support from Benson & Hedges and Mugen-Honda, Eddie Jordan's outfit has never looked so strong. The team is ready to become one of the leading lights of the next millennium.

Team *Jordan: On its way to glory*

Has its time come?

With an increased budget, experienced driver line-up and revised technical department, the team with the Irish spirit intends to build upon the impetus of last year's victory at Spa.

Fortified by his maiden grand prix victory last season, Eddie Jordan warns that he has now set fresh targets for his team. The next decade will belong to him, and he's convinced of as much. Why he is he so optimistic? He explained it all to us in detail, while at the same time touching on some of the things that have gone before...

"In our early days, in 1991," he says, "our first objective was to finish races, and once we'd done that we wanted to score points. No sooner had we managed one thing than we'd set ourselves a new goal. Pole positions, podiums...our progress was fairly consistent up until our first victory at Spa-Francorchamps last year.

A Jordan one-two

"Spa has always been a good circuit to us: that's where we clinched our F3 and F3000 titles with Johnny Herbert and Jean Alesi. No question, this momentous result – and you mustn't forget that Ralf Schumacher made it a one-two – has put us in a different position. The 1998 season brought us two essential things: a first win and a hitherto unknown level of confidence about the future. Now we know we have what it takes to

fight for a place in the top four of the championship."

Does that mean we should henceforth rank Jordan as one of the major players?

"Two years ago I would have said 'yes' without hesitation," he replies, "but now I'm not too sure what to think. I have completely different ideas on the subject. What I do know is that, this year, we have built the best car in our history. For 1999 we decided to restructure our approach completely. In our entire F1 history

we have never before launched a car so late. And that's a risk we took because we had absolute faith in what we had designed and built. Rather than investing time on testing and development, we decided to ensure that our design

and production were of the finest quality. To take that kind of risk you need great self-belief and total faith in your resources, I can assure you."

But that confidence can have its price, which in Eddie's case was the sale during the winter of a 40

An emblematic figurehead, Eddie Jordan has made constant progress since 1991.

Jordan likes to cultivate a fun image...though that doesn't dull its competitive edge.

All guns blazing, Jordan has greater expectations than ever before as it heads into the 1999 championship. The hornet has had a real taste for victory since Spa last year.

per cent stake in the team to American investment bank Warburg Pincus.

The last family team

"To understand why we did that," he says, "you have to look in several directions at the same time. Firstly, Jordan GP was the last F1 team to be owned and controlled by just one family, and I felt the time was right to build a stronger financial platform. I didn't want to be worrying about the money side of the business which, as I said, was entirely under my control before. Furthermore, by selling shares to a partner as strong as Warburg Pincus, I was not only providing future security for the team but I was aligning myself with a company that offers a wealth of possibilities and contacts."

Boosted by this fresh injection of capital, the team boss decided to start with a clean sheet, with fresh ambitions and new personnel. After 10 years with Jordan, meanwhile, the team's long-standing designer Gary Anderson, part of the set-up since the beginning, decided to leave.

"That was regrettable," says Jordan. "Gary and I have been friends for more than 20 years, and more to the point we still are, happily. But after a decade at the head of the team's technical division, there is no doubt that the time was ripe for him to change. To my mind, Gary Anderson is the most gifted engineer currently maturing in F1. He's a great designer, someone who understands exactly how a single-seater works but who, to my mind, is better still at making things happen. An ex-mechanic, he appreciates the technical heart of a car and he knows what is needed for it to function at its best. The downside, which is typical of the best guys in this business, is that he always wants to do everything himself; and in the end that can wind up aggravating some of the upcoming young engineers working with him."

Switched-on personnel

"Perhaps, in the end, his reputation and strength of character slightly stifled a department where there should be a free flow of ideas and initiatives. Formula One is becoming an ever more scientific business which requires personnel who are particularly switched on to their own specific responsibilities, aerodynamic or otherwise. Technology has moved on at such a pace that it's no longer possible to be a master of all things. With this in mind, I would have preferred it if Gary had become a kind of orchestra conductor, the man who ran and co-ordinated the technical department. But that wasn't what he wanted. Deep inside, Gary and I share the same ideas. We both prefer the idea of a small family team to a huge enterprise with 200 staff that modern F1 teams have become. Sadly, however, you have to move with the times. I'm sorry he's gone, but I'd prefer to see him happy elsewhere [at Stewart] than unhappy with us."

Anderson is not the only key figure to have left since last year. Gone, too, is the highly promising Ralf Schumacher, who has taken a

plum drive with Williams. In his place Jordan chose Heinz-Harald Frentzen, a decision that surprised many people. This flew in the face of the team's past habit of favouring youth over experience. What was the thinking behind it?

Crucial experience

"The answer to that question," says Eddie, "is Damon Hill. He showed us last year that experience is vital. Heinz-Harald has won a grand prix, has taken pole positions and has finished second in the world championship. He knows what we have to do if we are to achieve our targets. Traditionally Jordan has worked with young drivers, has educated them and has received a transfer fee when they have moved on to other teams. Indirectly, Ferrari paid for our wind tunnel facility when they purchased Eddie Irvine's contract from us. It was the same with Benetton and Fisichella. This is partly how we have financed some of the technical resources we have at our disposal, but we are no longer in a position where we need

to do that. We no longer have to let our major assets leave. We have a good budget, a good engine and two drivers who are fast and experienced in equal measure...In short, it's one of the best packages we have ever had.

"From now, my aim is to finish in the top three of the constructors' championship while staying in the

title hunt for as long as possible. In the final analysis it looks hard to beat McLaren and Ferrari, perhaps even impossible, but we have to maintain our progress. To finish third in the championship would be a good result, and we want to pick up a few victories along the way, of course. Me, I can't enough of days like Spa."

With a bigger budget and stronger technical resources, the Silverstone-based mob are gunning for a top three place in the constructors' championship.

Jordan's long-standing technical director Gary Anderson has transferred to Stewart GP and his place has been taken by Mike Gascoyne, one of the most prominent young engineers in the F1 paddock.

In Melbourne, the fanciful dream of Jacques Villeneuve, Craig Pollock and Adrian Reynard became reality. They had first discussed it on the eve of the Canadian's victory in the 1995 Indianapolis 500.

After a winter's efforts disrupted by the argument between BAR and the FIA over double livery on their cars, the BAR PR01, né Reynard, made a promising start in Australia.

F1 is his ultimate challenge.

Reynard Racing Cars... or BAR's secret weapon

Adrian Reynard

F1 is his ultimate challenge.

BAR's technical arm

Just 20 years ago a small company called Sabre Automotive was able to get by with a staff of 10. This was the ancestor of Reynard Racing Cars which, today, has some 500 people (including BAR personnel) working in its brand-new Brackley premises that incorporate various workshops and design studios. Here's a brief history of British American Racing's technical arm...

Birth of Sabre
In the early Seventies a young apprentice on secondment to British Leyland was pre-occupied with his final college project. So as not to upset his tutors, he gave his project a mildly misleading technical name, but the truth was that Adrian Reynard was building his first Formula Ford chassis.

In 1972, Reynard was made a proposal by Bill Stone, an acquaintance who was then production manager at March Engineering but who was known to be keen to branch out on his own. To 22-year-old Adrian's surprise the company would be owned 50/50 and in February 1973 Sabre Automotive was born.

The experienced Kiwi contributed £30 and Reynard donated his soldering iron. Sabre (Stone, Adrian, Bill, Reynard plus E for engineering) moved into premises in St John Street, Bicester, and in 1975 they entered the world of racing car manufacture by building five single-seaters, to which a further six were added the following year. By 1978 production

had increased to 20 units per annum, but Stone decided at that point to return to New Zealand and Adrian, a touch concerned, was left in sole charge. By chance, the following year he (literally) bumped into a certain Rick Gorne during a race at Thruxton.

Sabre becomes Reynard
After a stormy conversation they subsequently became pals for life and when Gorne found himself without the means to continue his own racing career, it was natural that Reynard turned to him. It was

a good move for Adrian, because Rick has an aptitude for business and management. By the beginning of 1980 the small St John Street workshops were becoming too

small and the team of 10 moved into an industrial unit on the edge of town. By 1983 the company was 10 years old and it was time for a fresh outlook: Sabre changed its name to Reynard.

It wasn't long before there were five industrial units as Reynard's core business gained satellite interests. "We had Reynard Racing Cars and Reynard Manufacturing

From left to right, Jacques Villeneuve, Rick Gorne, Craig Pollock, Adrian Reynard, Malcolm Oastler and Ricardo Zonta. The BAR F1 adventure is primed for launch.

113

operating out of three units," says the company co-founder, "to which we later added Reynard Special Vehicle Projects and Reynard Aviation." The first of these worked on any business not bearing the Reynard name, such as the Ford touring car project or the Panoz GT racer. The second was launched in partnership with the Virgin group, and specialised in aeronautical research. Having finally outgrown Bicester, however, it was time to move to Brackley.

BAR moves in

The new facility was opened amid pomp and ceremony on 8 July 1998 and Reynard's 280 personnel moved in along with the 220 from British American Racing. The new premises are well organised, with a wide central avenue that allows direct access to the various parts of the business. Spread out left and right you'll find Reynard Aviation, RSVP and Reynard Composites adjacent to the main manufacturing facility. And then, at last, you reach the most imposing building in the complex, grand but functional: the headquarters of BAR. It has been deliberately set apart to underline its total autonomy.

BAR is not Reynard and there is striking evidence of as much. On one side there is a chassis assembly area with seven bays, one for each car that will be built during the course of the F1 season. Further along are the research and development and composite facilities, and in the same area there is a suspension-testing appliance. Showers, cloakrooms and canteen are grouped together above the main thoroughfare. Behind the main building is a wind tunnel, while the press and marketing departments are located on the first floor, accessible via stairs from the main reception area. The design, engineering and team manager's offices are also up here. The administrative staff and directors are on the second floor.

Two separate businesses

At the hub, Adrian Reynard has an imperious view of the whole complex, as his interests are not merely limited to British American Racing. There are two separate businesses, but they both rely to a large extent on the experience and ability of Reynard. There are exchanges of information between various technical departments of BAR and Reynard (e.g. design and

French-Canadian Jacques Villeneuve, world champion in 1997, has taken up the biggest challenge of his career by joining BAR. As for Ricardo Zonta, there could be no better place for him to start out in F1 – and he didn't do a bad job in Melbourne.

After having captured most of the media attention during the winter, BAR fell back in line in Australia. The main priority now is hard work.

Luck plays a part in Formula One...Adrian Reynard and Craig Pollock will need a bit if their bold initiative is to succeed.

manufacture) and Adrian Reynard does not attempt to hide the fact. "Of course we swap information," he says, "because I negotiated a deal for Reynard to carry out some research work on BAR's behalf. It's obvious that the work we do is not just beneficial to British American Racing, it can also assist Reynard." Now, from its new site in Brackley, the Reynard group faces the toughest challenge of its 25-year existence. That's why the whole company had its eyes riveted on Melbourne on 7 March 1999. And it's certain that Adrian and loyal colleagues from the early days will have reflected just for a moment on the month of February 1973, when it all began.

THE KEY MEN...*Adrian's lieutenants*

RICK GORNE
It was during a Formula Ford race at Thruxton in 1977 that Adrian Reynard first came across Rick Gorne, who was born in Scunthorpe in July 1954. In 1982 he became Adrian's ninth employee and his sound business sense swiftly reaped rewards. In 1990 and 1996 Reynard was awarded Queen's Awards for Export. Now commercial director of British American Racing, he plays an important role, as his responsibilities encompass sponsorship, marketing, logistics, recruitment, supplier liaison, contract negotiations and factory development.

MALCOLM OASTLER
Born in 1960 in Sydney, Oastler picked up a diploma at the New South Wales University of Technology. He raced Formula Ford cars for two years in his homeland before setting out for England in February 1985. Approached by Reynard during that year's Formula Ford Festival, he went on to work on the company's 1986 model and was put in charge of the following year's Formula Ford design programme. He was responsible for the first-ever Reynard F3000 car, which Johnny Herbert took to victory on its debut in 1988, and he scored a repeat success six years later when Reynard won its first Indycar race. Although he has had several approaches from F1 and CART teams, he has always stayed loyal to Reynard because he appreciates the quality of life it gives him. Now chief designer for BAR, it has been his onerous responsibility to prepare the company's first F1 challenger.

Grands Prix

Australian Grand Prix
Melbourne
SUNDAY 7 MARCH 1999

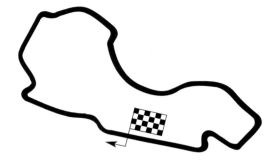

ADDRESS: Albert Park
Grand Prix Circuit,
Melbourne, Victoria 3205,
Australia

Tel:
00 61 3 92 58 71 00
Fax:
00 61 3 96 99 37 27

At the end of the 1996 season, after a decade of good, loyal service, South Australian capital Adelaide relinquished its right to stage a grand prix and handed the reins to its powerful neighbour Victoria. Since then the Formula One circus has adapted to the new location without fuss. The Albert Park circuit is in a charming spot, and in its early days it was the subject of vociferous opposition from environmental groups. The opposition has gradually faded, however, and there has never been any doubt that the vast majority of the population were in favour of the grand prix.

1998 podium:
- 1 Hakkinen (McLaren-Mercedes)
- 2 Coulthard (McLaren-Mercedes)
- 3 Frentzen (Williams-Mécachrome)

1998 statistics:
Pole position: 1m 30.010s, Hakkinen (McLaren-Mercedes)
Fastest race lap:
1m 31.649s (average 208.303km/h), Hakkinen (McLaren-Mercedes)

START : 14.00, local time (05.00 in Britain).
58 laps of a 5.302km circuit, total distance 307.52km

OLIVIER PANIS ON
MELBOURNE

Opinion: « It's always a pleasant place to be, even if it means a long time away from home. The track tends to be very dirty and lacks grip when we first venture out, but that's because it's not a permanent facility. There are no outstanding features, but there's usually something going on because there are several possible overtaking spots. »

Hot spot: « The series of bends after the main straight require several changes of direction at high speed. »

RACE HISTORY
First running: 1985
There have been 14 races in all,
11 at Adelaide and 3 at Melbourne
The previous 10 winners:
1998: Hakkinen (McLaren-Mercedes)
1997: Coulthard (McLaren-Mercedes)
1996: Hill (Williams-Renault)
1995: Hill (Williams-Renault)
1994: Mansell (Williams-Renault)
1993: Senna (McLaren-Ford)
1992: Berger (McLaren-Honda)
1991: Senna (McLaren-Honda)
1990: Piquet (Benetton-Ford)
1989: Boutsen (Williams-Renault)

RACE HISTORY

First running: 1973
There have been 26 races in all,
16 at SãoPaulo/Interlagos and 10 at Rio/Jacarepagua
The previous 10 winners:
1998: Hakkinen (McLaren-Mercedes)
1997: Villeneuve (Williams-Renault)
1996: Hill (Williams-Renault)
1995: M. Schumacher (Benetton-Renault)
1994: M. Schumacher (Benetton-Ford)
1993: Senna (McLaren-Ford)
1992: Mansell (Williams-Renault)
1991: Senna (McLaren-Honda)
1990: Prost (Ferrari)
1989: Mansell (Ferrari)

OLIVIER PANIS ON
INTERLAGOS

Opinion: « This is one of my favourites, even though it is the only anti-clockwise track on the calendar. It is very hard work physically, but it's the perfect place to test yourself to the maximum. I also like it for sentimental reasons, because I made my F1 debut here in 1994. »

Hot spot: « The uphill left-hander which precedes the drop onto the main straight. It might seem fairly straight if you walk along it, but it doesn't half feel like a corner when you go through at 300km/h. »

START: 13.00, local time (18.00 in Britain).
72 laps of a 4.259km circuit, total distance 307.075km

Grande Premio do Brasil

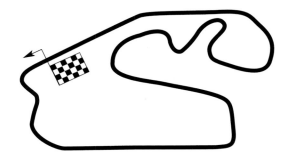

Brazilian Grand Prix
Interlagos

SUNDAY 11 APRIL 1999

Address: Autodromo
 José Carlos Pace,
Avenida Senator Teotonio Vilela 261,
São Paulo, Brazil

Tel:
00 55 11 521 99 11
Fax:
00 55 11 247 37 66

1998 podium:
- 1 Hakkinen (McLaren-Mercedes)
- 2 Coulthard (McLaren-Mercedes)
- 3 Schumacher M. (Ferrari)

1998 statistics:
Pole position: 1m 17.092s, Hakkinen (McLaren-Mercedes)
Fastest race lap: 1m 19.337s (average 194.754km/h), Hakkinen (McLaren-Mercedes)

Located 16km from the centre of the São Paulo metropolis, with its 20 million inhabitants, the Interlagos track features one of the starkest contrasts you will find anywhere in the world championship. Although it is sited in one of the richer city suburbs, impoverished shanty towns have still sprouted up nearby. The circuit fell out of public favour a little following the death of Ayrton Senna, but the nation has now overcome some of its sense of loss and the crowds are filtering back. To the rhythm of the samba, they cheer on the exploits of Rubens Barrichello, Pedro Diniz and Ricardo Zonta, from whom they are already expecting great things.

119

San Marino Grand Prix
Imola

Gran Premio di San Marino

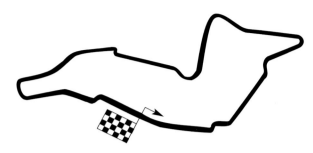

SUNDAY 2 MAY 1999

ADDRESS: Autodromo
Enzo e Dino Ferrari,
Via Fratelli Rosselli 2,
40026 IMOLA (Bologna), Italy

Tel :
00 39 0542 31 444
Fax :
00 39 0542 30 420

Located 35km to the south-east of Bologna, this marks the traditional starting point for the European season after the flyaway races in Australia and South America. Having spent a time living out of boxes, the world of F1 returns here to its opulent motorhomes. Although the surrounding countryside is magnificent, Imola tugs at the heartstrings whenever you go there because it is hard to forget the terrible grand prix weekend of 1994 that cost the lives of Roland Ratzenberger and Ayrton Senna.

START: 14.00, local time (13.00 in Britain).
62 laps of a 4.930km circuit, total distance 305.437km

1998 podium:
- **1** Coulthard (McLaren-Mercedes)
- **2** Schumacher M. (Ferrari)
- **3** Irvine (Ferrari)

1998 statistics:
Pole position: 1m 25.973s, Coulthard (McLaren-Mercedes)
Fastest race lap: 1m 29.345s (average 198.645 km/h), Schumacher M. (Ferrari)

OLIVIER PANIS ON
IMOLA

Opinion: « I don't like this race, doubtless because Senna was killed here when I was taking part in only my third grand prix. I had done well here in the past, though, and I qualified second in 1997. It's a nice circuit, though it doesn't fire me up a great deal. The atmosphere is good – but it's just not Monza. »

Hot spot: « The quick downhill section which precedes a steep climb. »

RACE HISTORY
First running: 1981.
There have been 18 races in all
The previous 10 winners:
1998: Coulthard (McLaren-Mercedes)
1997: Frentzen (Williams-Renault)
1996: Hill (Williams-Renault)
1995: Hill (Williams-Renault)
1994: M. Schumacher (Benetton-Renault)
1993: Prost (Williams-Renault)
1992: Mansell (Williams-Renault)
1991: Senna (McLaren-Honda)
1990: Patrese (Williams-Renault)
1989: Senna (McLaren-Honda)

Monaco Grand Prix
Grand Prix de Monaco
Monte-Carlo

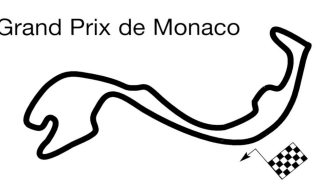

SUNDAY 16 MAY 1999

ADDRESS:
Automobile Club de Monaco,
23 Bd Albert 1er,
98012 Monaco Cedex

Tel:
00 377 93 15 26 00
Fax :
00 377 93 25 80 08

The jewel in the crown of world championship motor racing takes place in the principality of Monaco, 18km east of Nice. It stands out from all other grands prix because of an urban setting that, strictly speaking, flaunts Formula One's sporting code. Glamour, money, celebrities...it is the most fashionable gathering of the year. But while there are some spectacular sights in the paddock, there are none to match those on the track. Every driver has strong feelings about Monaco: they either like it or loathe it. Nelson Piquet was fond of saying that racing at Monaco was like trying to cycle round your living room – but he added that a win here was worth two anywhere else.

START: 14.00, local time (13.00 in Britain).
78 laps of a 3.367km circuit, total distance 262.626km

1998 podium:
• **1** Hakkinen (McLaren-Mercedes)
• **2** Fisichella (Benetton-Mécachrome)
• **3** Irvine (Ferrari)

1998 statistics:
Pole position: 1m 19.798s, Hakkinen (McLaren-Mercedes)
Fastest race lap:
1m 22.948s (average 146.130 km/h), Hakkinen (McLaren-Mercedes)

OLIVIER PANIS ON *MONACO*

Opinion: « I love Monaco – and not just because I scored my only F1 win here. I've always gone quite well on this circuit. I love the atmosphere too, it's a really vibrant event. It's a great sensation to be so close to the crowd, to feel their presence. »
Hot spot: « No question, Casino Square and the exit from the tunnel are both absolutely epic. »

RACE HISTORY:
First running: 1929.
There have been 45 races since the creation of the world championship in 1950
The previous 10 winners:
1998: Hakkinen (McLaren-Mercedes)
1997: M. Schumacher (Ferrari)
1996: Panis (Ligier-Mugen-Honda)
1995: M. Schumacher (Benetton-Renault)
1994: M. Schumacher (Benetton-Ford)
1993: Senna (McLaren-Ford)
1992: Senna (McLaren-Honda)
1991: Senna (McLaren-Honda)
1990: Senna (McLaren-Honda)
1989: Senna (McLaren-Honda)

Gran Premio de España

Spanish Grand Prix
Barcelona
SUNDAY 30 MAY 1999

ADDRESS: Circuit de Catalunya, Km 2,
Carretera de Granollers,
Montmello,
Barcelona, Spain

Tel:
00 34 9 35 71 97 00
Fax:
00 34 9 35 72 30 61

The circuit, 20km north of Barcelona, was developed on the back of the financial impetus that accompanied preparations for the 1992 Olympic Games. Christened the Circuit of Catalunya, it meets all modern F1 criteria, with an enormous pit complex and big run-off areas. And unlike Magny-Cours, the track's developers have given it some character thanks to an undulating, challenging layout that appeals to drivers and fans alike. Its location and clement weather also make it the capital of winter testing.

START : 14.00, local time (13.00 in Britain).
65 laps of a 4.728km circuit, total distance 307.152km

1998 podium:
- 1 Hakkinen (McLaren-Mercedes)
- 2 Coulthard (McLaren-Mercedes)
- 3 Schumacher M. (Ferrari)

1998 statistics
Pole position: 1m 29.262s, Hakkinen (McLaren-Mercedes)
Fastest race lap: 1m 24.275s (average 201.967km/h), Hakkinen (McLaren-Mercedes)

OLIVIER PANIS ON
BARCELONA

Opinion : «Even though we spend a lot of time there during the year, I like it a lot. It's a nice place to work. The weather is often good and the track is fantastic, with ample run-off areas. On the other hand, however, it's probably not the best for spectators.»

Hot spot : « The quick right leading onto the pit straight looks quite tight – but imagine coming through at 210km/h, flat out in fourth gear. By the end of the straight we are touching 305km/h! »

RACE HISTORY
First running: 1951
There have been 28 races in all,
2 at Pedrables, 9 at Jarama, 4 at Montjuich, 5 at Jerez and 8 at Barcelona
The previous 10 winners:
1998: Hakkinen (McLaren-Mercedes)
1997: Villeneuve (Williams-Renault;
1996: M. Schumacher (Ferrari)
1995: M. Schumacher (Benetton-Renault)
1994: Hill (Williams-Renault)
1993: Prost (Williams-Renault)
1992: Mansell (Williams-Renault)
1991: Mansell (Williams-Renault)
1990: Senna (McLaren-Honda)
1989: Senna (McLaren-Honda)

Grand Prix du Canada

1998 podium:
- 1 Schumacher M. (Ferrari)
- 2 Fisichella (Benetton-Mécachrome)
- 3 Irvine (Ferrari)

1998 statistics:
Pole position: 1m 18.213s, Coulthard (McLaren-Mercedes)
Fastest race lap: 1m 19.379s (average 200.501km/h), Schumacher M. (Ferrari)

Canadian Grand Prix
Montreal

SUNDAY 13 JUNE 1999

ADDRESS: Circuit Gilles Villeneuve,
Tour de contrôle, Ile notre Dame,
Montreal, Quebec H3C 4O,
Canada

Tel:
00 1 514 350 47 31
Fax:
00 1 514 350 00 07

This is one of the most popular events of the season, thanks to the warm welcome of Quebec, the general charms of North America – and the fact the race is usually exciting. Spectators come to the race by public transport because it's only a few kilometres from the city centre, on the Ile Notre Dame that has previously staged the World Exhibition and several Olympic events. It's hard to escape from Villeneuve mania, such is the esteem in which Gilles and Jacques are held locally – though you can always get away for a while by nipping off to the shops.

START: 13.00, local time (18.00 in Britain).
69 laps of a 4.421km circuit, total distance 305.049km

RACE HISTORY
First running: 1967
There have been 30 races in all,
8 at Mosport, 2 at Mont-Tremblant and 20 at Montreal
The previous 10 winners:
1998: M. Schumacher (Ferrari)
1997: M. Schumacher (Ferrari)
1996: Hill (Williams-Renault)
1995: Alesi (Ferrari)
1994: M. Schumacher (Benetton-Ford)
1993: Prost (Williams-Renault)
1992: Berger (McLaren-Honda)
1991: Piquet (Benetton-Ford)
1990: Senna (McLaren-Honda)
1989: Boutsen (Williams-Renault)

OLIVIER PANIS ON
MONTREAL

Opinion: « I didn't like this track even before I had my bad accident there in 1997. I do love the country, however. The people make you ever so welcome and they are really switched on about the sport. Their enthusiasm compensates for a boring track, which is just an endless series of chicanes. »
Hot spot: « The place where I had my crash, between Turns Four and Five, and the end of the long straight before the pits. »

French Grand Prix
Magny-Cours

Grand Prix de France

SUNDAY 27 JUNE 1999

ADDRESS: Circuit de Nevers-Magny-Cours,
Technopole,
58470 Magny-Cours,
France

Tel:
00 33 3 86 21 80 00
Fax:
00 33 3 86 21 81 41

The Nivernais circuit has an advantageous location, 250km south of Paris, 12km south of Nevers and 220km north of Lyon. But that's the only good thing to be said for it. It's cold, impersonal and embodies all that's worst about the antiseptic tracks of the modern day. It's a perfect illustration of how not to do things and is the least popular place on the world championship calendar in every respect. It's dull for the driver and visitors don't find the region terribly welcoming. It's a pity, because in the old days Magny-Cours was the absolute bedrock of French motor sport.

1998 podium:
- **1** Schumacher M. (Ferrari)
- **2** Irvine (Ferrari)
- **3** Hakkinen (McLaren-Mercedes)

1998 statistics:
Pole position: 1m 14.929s, Hakkinen (McLaren-Mercedes)
Fastest race lap: 1m 17.523s (average 197.360km/h), Coulthard (McLaren-Mercedes)

START: 14.00, local time
(13.00 in Britain).
72 laps of a 4.250km circuit, total distance 305.84km

RACE HISTORY
First running: 1950
There have been 48 races in all,
11 at Reims, 4 at Clermont-Ferrand, 1 at Le Mans, 14 at the Paul Ricard, 5 at Dijon and 8 at Magny-Cours
Previous 10 winners:
1998: M. Schumacher (Ferrari)
1997: M. Schumacher (Ferrari)
1996: Hill (Williams-Renault)
1995: M. Schumacher
 (Benetton-Renault)
1994: M. Schumacher
 (Benetton-Ford)
1993: Prost (Williams-Renault)
1992: Mansell (Williams-Renault)
1991: Mansell (Williams-Renault)
1990: Prost (Ferrari).
1989: Prost (McLaren-Honda)

OLIVIER PANIS ON
MAGNY-COURS
Opinion: « It's my national circuit, not a good place to do much work, because it's not ideal for evolving new set-ups, but I do like it. I also lived in Magny-Cours for a while. It is one of the safest tracks in the world, too, with huge run-off areas. It's also a circuit with plenty of grip. »
Hot spot: « The Nürburgring and Imola chicanes give you a real buzz. »

RACE HISTORY

First running: 1950
There have been 49 races in all,
32 at Silverstone, 5 at Aintree, 12 at Brands Hatch
The previous 10 winners:
1998: Schumacher M. (Ferrari)
1997: Villeneuve J. (Williams-Renault)
1996: Villeneuve J. (Williams-Renault)
1995: Herbert (Benetton-Renault)
1994: Hill (Williams-Renault)
1993: Prost (Williams-Renault)
1992: Mansell (Williams-Renault)
1991: Mansell (Williams-Renault)
1990: Prost (Ferrari)
1989: Prost (McLaren-Honda)

OLIVIER PANIS ON
SILVERSTONE

Opinion: « The circuit has changed a great deal in recent years and some legendary corners have been sacrificed in the name of safety. Even so, it is still physically demanding and requires total commitment from the driver. It's a real bastion of Formula One and the crowd here is particularly well informed. »
Hot spot: « Becketts – plus all the places where you are in fifth or sixth gear. Very impressive. »

START: 14.00. 60 laps of a 5.140km circuit, total distance 308.229km

British Grand Prix
Silverstone
SUNDAY 11 JULY 1999

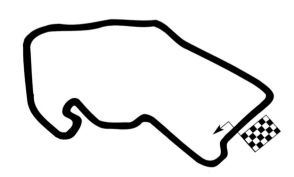

1998 podium:
- 1 Schumacher M. (Ferrari)
- 2 Hakkinen (McLaren-Mercedes)
- 3 Irvine (Ferrari)

1998 statistics:
Pole position: 1m 23.271s, Hakkinen
(McLaren-Mercedes)
Fastest race lap: 1m 35.704s (average
193.346km/h) in rain, Hakkinen
(McLaren-Mercedes)

ADDRESS: Silverstone Circuits Ltd,
Silverstone, near Towcester,
Northamptonshire NN12 8TN,
England

Tel:
0132 785 7271
Fax :
0132 785 7663

Silverstone has the same kind of allure as Indianapolis, in America, or Le Mans, in France. The name is recognised throughout the world as a racing Mecca. Situated 110km north of London, 25km south-east of Northampton and 45km from Oxford, it is nicknamed the "Home of British Motor Racing". And with good reason, too, as it was here in 1948 that a disused airfield was converted to help kick-start motor sport after the Second World War. F1's so-called "Silicone Valley" has grown up around Silverstone, such is the number of sub-contractors in the region. In short, you go to Silverstone with much the same approach that you go to church: with devotion.

Austrian Grand Prix
A-1 Ring

SUNDAY 25 JULY 1999

ADDRESS:
Ring Management Gmbh.,
8724 Spielberg,
Austria

Tel:
00 43 357 77 53
Fax:
00 43 357 77 10

Grosser Preiss von Osterreich

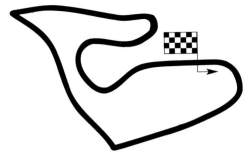

The A1-Ring is fairly new – built on the site of the classic old Osterreichring, 200km west of Vienna and about half as far from Graz. It is only a pale imitation of its famous forebear, though some of the strong points have been retained. The developers have preserved a countryside atmosphere among the sweeping greenery of the Styrian foothills, even though the track no longer winds its way through the pine forests. The track is in a concentrated area that gives spectators an unrivalled view.

START : 14.00, local time (13.00 in Britain).
71 laps of a 4.319km circuit, total distance 306.649km

1998 podium:
• **1** Hakkinen (McLaren-Mercedes)
• **2** Coulthard (McLaren-Mercedes)
• **3** Schumacher M. (Ferrari)

1998 statistics:
Pole position: 1m 29.598s, Fisichella (Benetton-Mécachrome) on a wet surface
Fastest race lap: 1m 12.878s (average 213.348km/h), Coulthard (McLaren-Mercedes)

OLIVIER PANIS ON
the A-1 RING

Opinion: « This was new to me last season because in 1997 my legs were in plaster. It's not a very inspiring track – a repetitive sequence of brake, hairpin and straight. But the rural atmosphere is a breath of fresh air. It's a charming country. »
Hot spot: « You can brake very late at the end of the ascent to the second corner, and the next bend is quite a challenge, too. »

RACE HISTORY
First running: 1964
There have been 21 races in all, 18 at Zeltweg, 1 on the Osterreichring and 2 on the A1-Ring.
The previous 10 winners:
1998: Hakkinen (McLaren-Mercedes)
1997: Villeneuve (Williams-Renault)
1987: Mansell (Williams-Honda)
1986: Prost (McLaren-TAG)
1985: Prost (McLaren-TAG)
1984: Lauda (McLaren-TAG)
1983: Prost (Renault)
1982: De Angelis (Lotus-Ford)
1981: Laffite (Ligier-Matra)
1980: Jabouille (Renault)

German Grand Prix
Hockenheim

SUNDAY 1 AUGUST 1999

ADDRESS: Hockenheimring,
Postfach 1106,
D-68754 Hockenheim,
Germany

Tel:
00 49 62 05 95 00.
Fax:
00 49 62 05 95 02

Hockenheim is unique, with its enormous stadium and interminable straights that cut dark channels through the middle of the forest. It lies 90km south of Frankfurt, 110km north-east of Stuttgart and about 20km from the historic city of Heidelberg – and it's a worthy descendant of Germany's pre-war circuits. It's a true temple of speed where engine performance is critical. For safety reasons the track now features three chicanes, but it's still a place where mechanical components are strained to their limit.

START: 14.00, local time (13.00 in Britain).
45 laps of a 6.823km circuit, total distance 307.022km

1998 podium:
- **1** Hakkinen (McLaren-Mercedes)
- **2** Coulthard (McLaren-Mercedes)
- **3** Villeneuve J. (Williams-Mécachrome)

1998 statistics:
Pole position: 1m 41.838s, Hakkinen (McLaren-Mercedes)
Fastest race lap: 1m 46.116s (average 231.471km/h), Coulthard (McLaren-Mercedes)

RACE HISTORY
First running: 1951
There have been 46 races in all, 23 at the Nürburgring, 22 at Hockenheim and 1 at Avus-Berlin
The previous 10 winners:
1998: Hakkinen (McLaren-Mercedes)
1997: Berger (Benetton-Renault)
1996: Hill (Williams-Renault)
1995: M. Schumacher (Benetton-Renault)
1994: Berger (Ferrari)
1993: Prost (Williams-Renault)
1992: Mansell (Williams-Renault)
1991: Mansell (Williams-Renault)
1990: Senna (McLaren-Honda)
1989: Senna (McLaren-Honda)

OLIVIER PANIS ON
HOCKENHEIM

Opinion: « You always get a big crowd here but I don't share their enthusiasm for the place – even though I've done quite well in the past. I won an F3000 race here and it's also where I scored my first podium finish in F1. But I'm still not that keen. »

Hot spot: « The most impressive thing is coming into the stadium. You can really sense the spectators' presence – it's quite scary. That apart, the runs through the forest aren't bad either. »

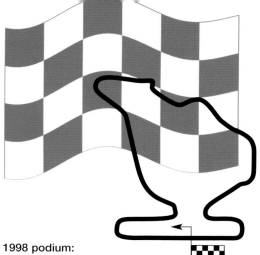

Hungarian Grand Prix
Hungaroring

SUNDAY 15 AUGUST 1999

ADDRESS: Hungaroring,
2146 Mogyorod,
PO Box 10,
Hungary

Tel:
00 36 28 444 444/113
Fax:
00 36 28 441 860/866

1998 podium:
• 1 Schumacher M. (Ferrari)
• 2 Coulthard (McLaren-Mercedes)
• 3 Villeneuve J. (Williams-Mécachrome)

1998 statistics:
Pole position: 1m 16.973s, Hakkinen (McLaren-Mercedes)
Fastest race lap: 1m 19.266s (average 182.379km/h), Schumacher M. (Ferrari)

The Hungarian Grand Prix always has something of a holiday atmosphere because of when it takes place and the fantastic weather in which mainland Europe is usually bathed. The track is 20km north-east of Budapest, close to the small town of Mogyorod. To everyone's delight the paddock mood is usually quite relaxed, because the extreme heat has a slightly somnolent effect. Perhaps it's because some people are slightly off their guard that a few daring transfer swoops are made – over the years some of the most spectacular deals have been signed in Budapest.

START: 14.00, local time (13.00 in Britain).
77 laps of a 3.972km circuit, total distance 305.536km

RACE HISTORY
First running: 1986
There have been 13 races in all
The previous 10 winners:
1998: M. Schumacher (Ferrari)
1997: Villeneuve (Williams-Renault)
1996: Villeneuve (Williams-Renault)
1995: Hill (Williams-Renault)
1994: M. Schumacher (Benetton-Ford)
1993: Hill (Williams-Renault)
1992: Senna (McLaren-Honda)
1991: Senna (McLaren-Honda)
1990: Boutsen (Williams-Renault)
1989: Mansell (Ferrari)

OLIVIER PANIS ON
BUDAPEST

Opinion: « It reminds me of Argentina in many ways. It could be a good circuit, but because the surface is so dirty not even three days of a grand prix weekend are enough to clean it. It is also very hard physically because it is so twisty. There's absolutely no chance to rest and you are never far away from making a mistake. »
Hot spot: « There's a series of chicanes on the opposite side of the circuit to the pits which are a challenge. The counterpoint is one particularly dismal downhill right-hander. »

Belgian Grand Prix
Grand Prix de Belgique
Spa-Francorchamps

SUNDAY 29 AUGUST 1999

ADDRESS: Circuit de Spa-Francorchamps,
Circuit House, Route du circuit 55,
B-4970 Francorchamps,
Belgium

Tel:
00 32 87 27 51 43
Fax:
00 32 87 27 55 51

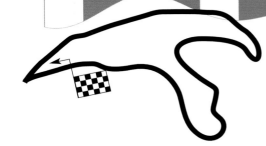

This is one track that brooks no argument. Lying 50km south-east of Liège and the same south-west of Aix-la-Chapelle, Germany, Spa is a legendary circuit that has been adapted without losing any of its character – unlike the Nürburgring or Austria. Although it is half the length it used to be, it is still utterly authentic and packed with names that are a part of racing folklore – Raidillon, Eau Rouge, Blanchimont...All represent a compelling challenge, no matter how much the circuit has been modified. Winding its way through the Belgian Ardennes, where the weather is prone to sudden change, Spa is a venue where only true champions can shine.

1998 podium:
• **1** Hill (Jordan-Mugen-Honda)
• **2** Schumacher R. (Jordan-Mugen-Honda)
• **3** Alesi (Sauber-Petronas)

1998 statistics:
Pole position: 1m 48.682s, Hakkinen (McLaren-Mercedes)
Fastest race lap: 2m 03.766s (average 202.679km/h) in rain, Schumacher M. (Ferrari)

START: 14.00, local time (13.00 in Britain).
44 laps of a 6.968km circuit, total distance 306.592km

OLIVIER PANIS ON
SPA

Opinion: « To most drivers, Spa is the finest track in the world. Its length, location and design combine to make it truly magical. The Raidillon demands great commitment and you think about it every lap, long before you get there. It's a place that sorts the men from the boys, but it's a pity we don't go through flat out with the current cars. »

Hot spot: « Raidillon, no question. You breathe a sigh of relief every time you come through intact. »

RACE HISTORY
First running: 1950
There have been 45 races in all, 33 at Spa-Francorchamps, 10 at Zolder and 2 at Nivelles
The previous 10 winners:
1998: Hill (Jordan-Mugen-Honda)
1997: M. Schumacher (Ferrari)
1996: M. Schumacher (Ferrari)
1995: M. Schumacher (Benetton-Renault)
1994: Hill (Williams-Renault)
1993: Hill (Williams-Renault)
1992: Schumacher M. (Benetton-Ford)
1991: Senna (McLaren-Honda)
1990: Senna (McLaren-Honda)
1989: Senna (McLaren-Honda)

Italian Grand Prix
Monza
SUNDAY 12 SEPTEMBER 1999

ADDRESS:
Autodromo Nazionale di Monza,
Parco Monza,
20052 Monza, Italy

Tel:
00 39 039 24 821
Fax:
00 39 039 32 324

Located in parkland just 15km north of Milan, this is a part of motor racing's rich heritage – along with Monaco, Silverstone, Spa and the Nürburgring. No other track has an atmosphere quite like it – and that's to do with Ferrari, the tifosi and Italy's unrivalled passion for the sport. Monza is more than a racing circuit, it's a shrine where fans come to pay their respects to motor racing in general (and the Prancing Horse in particular). When one of the famous red cars wins, the shrine becomes a cauldron and a red wave sweeps across the track. Magic!

Gran Premio d'Italia

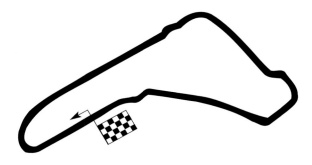

1998 podium:
• **1** Schumacher M. (Ferrari)
• **2** Irvine (Ferrari)
• **3** Schumacher R. (Jordan-Mugen-Honda)

1998 statistics:
Pole position: 1m 25.289s, Schumacher M. (Ferrari)
Fastest race lap: 1m 25.139s (average 243.977km/h), Hakkinen (McLaren-Mercedes)

START : 14.00, local time (13.00 in Britain).
53 laps of a 5.770km circuit, total distance 305.545km

OLIVIER PANIS ON
MONZA

Opinion: « I adore the place. It's fantastic to arrive at a corner like the Parabolica at more than 300km/h. The car understeers on the way in and then you fight to stick to the racing line to stop it oversteering. You really need your wits about you. And for atmosphere, there's nowhere like it. »

Hot spot: « Parabolica. You can pick up a lot of time there, but it's just as easy to lose a chunk, too. »

RACE HISTORY
First running: 1950
There have been 49 races in all,
48 at Monza and 1 at Imola
The previous 10 winners:
1998: M. Schumacher (Ferrari)
1997: Coulthard (McLaren-Mercedes)
1996: M. Schumacher (Ferrari)
1995: Herbert (Benetton-Renault)
1994: Hill (Williams-Renault)
1993: Hill (Williams-Renault)
1992: Senna (McLaren-Honda)
1991: Mansell (Williams-Renault)
1990: Senna (McLaren-Honda)
1989: Prost (McLaren-Honda)

RACE HISTORY
First running: 1983
There have been 9 races in all,
2 at Brands Hatch, 4 at the Nürburgring,
1 at Donington and 2 at Jerez
The previous 8 winners:
1997: Hakkinen (McLaren-Mercedes)
1996: Villeneuve (Williams-Renault)
1995: Schumacher M. (Benetton-Renault)
1994: Schumacher M. (Benetton-Ford)
1993: Senna (McLaren-Ford)
1985: Mansell (Williams-Honda turbo)
1984: Prost (McLaren-Honda turbo)
1983: Piquet (Brabham-BMW turbo)

OLIVIER PANIS ON
NÜRBURGRING
Opinion: « It's hard to overtake here in a race. And it's always cold, so it's tough getting tyres up to working temperature, which doesn't help. Even so I like driving here, despite the fact the weather usually does its worst. »

Hot spot: « There is a long downhill stretch at the end of which you brake very, very late. It reminds me of Nouveau Monde on the old Rouen-les-Essarts circuit, which was always fun. »

START: 14.00, local time (13.00 in Britain).
67 laps of a 4.556km circuit, total distance 305.252km

European Grand Prix
Nürburgring

SUNDAY 26 SEPTEMBER 1999

ADDRESS:
Nürburgring GmbH.,
D-5489 Nürburg/Eifel,
Germany

Tel:
00 49 26 91 30 20
Fax:
00 49 26 91 30 21 55

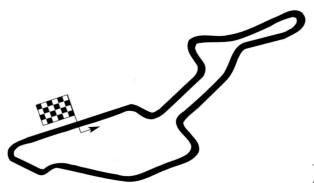

1998 podium:
(same venue, but called Luxembourg Grand Prix):
• 1 Hakkinen (McLaren-Mercedes)
• 2 Schumacher M. (Ferrari)
• 3 Coulthard (McLaren-Mercedes)

1998 statistics:
Pole position: 1m 18.561s, Schumacher M. (Ferrari)
Fastest race lap: 1m 20.450s (average 208.128km/h),
 Hakkinen (McLaren-Mercedes)

The original version of this legendary venue was lost to F1 after Niki Lauda's fiery accident in 1976. Drivers of the old school still talk about the 22.835km with a touch of fear in their eyes. That verdant roller coaster has now given way to a track devoid of any outstanding features. Where Spa succeeded, the Nürburgring – 60km east of Koblenz, 80km south of Cologne and 55km from Bonn – failed miserably. After staging the Luxembourg GP for two years, it reverts this season to hosting the Grand Prix of Europe. The name still attracts huge crowds, and any visitors who want to test themselves on the sleeping giant next door can do so for about 20 deutschmarks per lap. But be careful – it can still bite.

131

Malaysian Grand Prix
Sepang

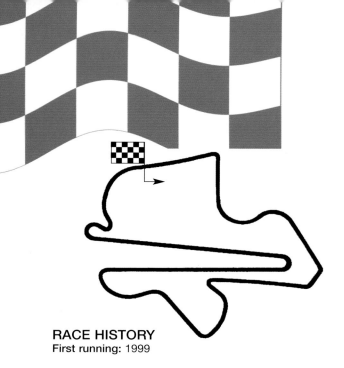

RACE HISTORY
First running: 1999

**Podiums and
Statistics:** Nothing yet!

SUNDAY 17 OCTOBER 1999

ADDRESS: Sepang International Circuit,
Wisma Bintang, Lot 13A, Jalan 225,
46100 Petaling Selangor,
Darul Ehsan, Malaysia

Tel:
00 603 755 55 55
Fax:
00 603 755 73 19

Although new to the calendar this year, the Malaysian GP is tipped to become one of the major attractions of the season. The venue's infrastructure and the quality of its facilities are said to surpass the required standards with ease. An hour by motorway from Kuala Lumpur – which shares with Hong Kong and Singapore the honour of being one of south-east Asia's most exciting cities – the Sepang circuit is the result of a burgeoning economy, the fruits of which most of the country is enjoying. A vibrant, ambitious country, Malaysia has created a circuit in its own image. It promises to be a good weekend.

START: 14.00, local time (07.00 in Britain).
56 laps of a 5.542km circuit, total distance 310.362km

OLIVIER PANIS ON
SEPANG
Opinion: « What can I say? The circuit is brand new and has never been used. I won't pass comment until I've tried it. »

Japanese Grand Prix
Suzuka

SUNDAY 31 OCTOBER 1999

ADDRESS: Suzuka International Racing Course,
7992 Ino-Cho, Suzuka-Shi,
Mie-Ken 510-02,
Japan

Tel:
00 81 593 70 14 65
Fax:
00 81 593 70 18 18

It's a bit like an army assault course trying to get there – 500km west of Tokyo, 150km east of Osaka and 70km south-west of Nagoya. It's owned by Honda, which uses it as a test track, and there's a big funfair alongside. The death of Ayrton Senna – regarded as a demi-god in Japan – deterred the crowds for a while, but they have now recovered their appetite for the sport. And Suzuka is another of F1's jewels. It's as demanding as Spa-Francorchamps and is often lauded by the drivers, who compliment the variety of its corners. In short, it's one of those you have to visit.

START: 14.00, local time (04.00 hours in Britain).
53 laps of a 5.864km circuit, total distance 310.582km

1998 podium:
• 1 Hakkinen (McLaren-Mercedes)
• 2 Irvine (Ferrari)
• 3 Coulthard (McLaren-Mercedes)

1998 statistics:
Pole position: 1m 36.293s, Schumacher M. (Ferrari)
Fastest race lap: 1m 40.190s (average 210.703km),
  Schumacher M. (Ferrari)

RACE HISTORY
First running: 1976
There have been 14 races in all,
2 at Mount Fuji and 12 at Suzuka
The previous 10 winners:
1998: Hakkinen (McLaren-Mercedes)
1997: M. Schumacher (Ferrari)
1996: Hill (Williams-Renault)
1995: M. Schumacher (Benetton-Renault)
1994: Hill (Williams-Renault)
1993: Senna (McLaren-Ford)
1992: Patrese (Williams-Renault)
1991: Berger (McLaren-Honda)
1990: Piquet (Benetton-Ford)
1989: Nannini (Benetton-Ford)

OLIVIER PANIS ON
SUZUKA

Opinion: « This is one of the best circuits in the world. You have to get into a good driving rhythm straight away, or you'll quickly be lulled into a mistake – and there are ample opportunities to make those. It's an excellent place to develop a car, and there is added interest because you can try out a number of different race strategies. »

Hot spot: « You have to attack the whole circuit, but the series of quick chicanes is particularly satisfying. »

Regulations – technical and sporting

What you need to know!
To understand racing strategy and fathom out what makes Formula One tick, even experts need to grasp a few basic rules. Here's a quick guided tour for fans...

Technical Regulations

Dimensions: There is a very dense technical manual that outlines what can and cannot be done to create an F1 car. The size and shape of virtually all components are very clearly defined and engineers are left with very little scope to produce something that looks different. The car's total weight, with driver on board, must be at least 600kg.

Engine: Maximum 3000cc, piston-operated four-stroke, no forced induction, a maximum of 12 cylinders (each with circular cross-section), no more than five valves per cylinder. Variable inlet trumpets are banned and crankshaft and camshafts must be forged from iron or steel. The use of composite materials is not permitted for pistons, head or cylinder block.

Fuel: The tank is a rubber bag specified by the FIA. There is no capacity limit and it must be contained within the central survival cell, between the driver's back and the engine. Standard pump fuel must be used and has to be stored at ambient temperature.

Transmission: At least two wheels must be driven, but four-wheel drive is banned. The gearbox has to have at least four forward speeds but no more than seven; a reverse gear must be fitted. Cars also have to be equipped with a device to enable the clutch to be disengaged when the engine is not running. Semi-automatic transmission is permissible, but traction control systems are not.

Suspension: F1 cars' suspension systems must be influenced only by the vertical loads to which the wheels are subjected. No electronic suspension control is allowed.

Steering: Cars must have a minimum of two wheels that steer, but four-wheel steering is outlawed. Power assistance may be used, so long as the system serves only to reduce physical effort on the driver's part.

Brakes: Each wheel is limited to a single caliper (with up to six pistons) and one disc (which must not exceed a certain size). All forms of ABS are banned. Dual circuit braking operated by a single pedal is mandatory.

Wheels and tyres: There must be four complete wheel and tyre units – no more, no less. These have to be located outside the bodywork. FIA-standard grooved tyres are compulsory and are subject to size restrictions. Wheel diameter should not exceed 330mm. Each car is limited to a maximum of 32 dry-weather tyres and 28 rain tyres per race weekend.

Safety: The cockpit and fuel tank are housed within a central safety cell that is subjected to a rigorous crash-testing procedure. There is a dual fire extinguisher system in the cockpit. This meets stringent standards in terms of the quantity and quality of its output: if needed, it simultaneously sprays an extinguishing agent towards both the engine and the cockpit. Cars must be fitted with internal and external cut-off switches that can be actuated by the driver or track marshals. There is a cockpit surround that offers the driver lateral and rearward head protection. A six-point harness is fitted (most road cars have only a three-point fixing) and the belts are 75mm wide. It is compulsory to have two rear-view mirrors and a rear light (red) that must be switched on in the event of rain. Steering wheels are fitted with a quick-release system and the four external wheels have a safety cable to prevent them becoming completely detached. An aircraft-style black box is used to measure vital data in event of an accident. The driver's apparel (helmet, overalls, underwear, gloves and socks) needs to be homologated and approved by the FIA and must provide a required standard of fire resistance.

TV cameras: FOCA selects cars to carry one or more live cameras. Those not equipped carry dummy units of the same size and weight.

Technical changes for 1999

- **The most important rule change concerns tyres.** The allocation of dry-weather tyres has been reduced from 40 to 32 per car during the course of a grand prix weekend; this is a corollary of a new, harder rubber compound. Also, like the rear tyres, the fronts now have a fourth groove (there were only three in 1998). A maximum width has also been set for front tyres, at 270mm.
- **The technical manual now specifies precisely** the extent of electronic or computer-controlled aids that can be used to help the driver. It addresses all relevant domains (engine, transmission, brakes and so on).
- **Drivers can now receive** direct information from track marshals via lights on their dash panel.
- **The other changes concern** a variety of technical topics: cooling system pressure is limited to 3.75 bars, front wings are now strength tested and there are rules governing seat installation and the position of bleed pipes.

Sporting Regulations

Entry: The world championship is open to drivers with the relevant F1 "superlicence". Teams may enter no more than two cars. During the course of a season, a team may nominate one change of driver for its lead car and up to three for its second (though exceptions can be made in cases of force majeure). All entered drivers will be eligible to score championship points.

Championship: This will comprise at least eight but no more than 17 grands prix. A race will last for however many laps it takes to cover 305km, but will not extend beyond two hours. To take part in the race, a driver must complete a qualifying lap within 107 per cent of the pole position time. Starting grid order will be determined by qualifying times, with the fastest car at the front and the slowest at the back.

Finish: The chequered flag will be shown after the completion of a pre-determined number of laps. If the flag is mistakenly shown too soon, the race will be deemed to have finished. If the flag is shown too late, however, the result will be taken from the lap on which the race was scheduled to end. All drivers who cross the finishing line will be classified, so long as they have completed at least 90 per cent of the number of laps covered by the winner. After crossing the line, drivers must head straight for *parc fermé* without stopping and without outside assistance (other than from marshals). All classified finishers will be subjected to a weight check. Championship points will be awarded to the top six finishers on a 10-6-4-3-2-1 sliding scale.

Sundries: Refuelling stops are permitted only in the pit lane and every team must use an identical FIA-approved rig. A top-up is allowed on the grid up to five minutes before the start, however, so long as a specified, 12-litre capacity churn is used. No oil may be added to a car during a race. Contact between driver, car and pits is allowed within certain parameters: pit boards and radios can be used, but telemetry data must be one way only – from car to pit. Spare chassis can be used during qualifying, but no change of car is allowed once the race has started. Pit lane speed limits apply – 80 km/h during practice and 120 km/h in the race.

Timetable: Scrutineering takes place from 10.00-18.00 on Thursday, when free practice will be arranged if a circuit is new to the championship. There is free practice from 11.00-12.00 and 13.00-14.00 on Friday (Thursday in Monaco). More follows on Saturday, from 09.00-09.45 and 10.15-11.00. The qualifying session is from 13.00-14.00 and drivers are permitted a maximum of 12 laps each. On Sunday, there is a 30-minute warm-up four-and a half hours before the scheduled start. Half an hour before the race, the pit lane opens to allow a few reconnaissance laps before cars take their grid slots. It closes 15 minutes before the start and cars yet to leave will be forced to start from the end of the pit lane once the others have gone. The grid is "closed" 10 minutes before the start and any cars not in place will be allowed to start only from the pits. With five minutes to go, the official countdown begins, a series of boards showing 3 minutes, 1 minute, 30 seconds etc. At the appointed time a green flag signals a final warm-up lap (any competitors in trouble now will be sent to the back of the grid, or the pits). Once the cars have returned and are in place and stationary, five red lights come on at one-second intervals. When the lights go off, that's the signal to start.

Black box: Since 1998 F1 cars have been fitted with accident data recorders that record vital information before and during any incident. Data is logged 1000 times per second.

New sporting regulations for 1999

- **A maximum of 24 cars** (12 teams) will be admitted to the championship. Previously there had been no limits, and in the past pre-qualifying sessions used to be arranged to reduce the entry to a manageable level.
- **Following a deal between teams** (and not as the result of an FIA directive), testing is restricted to 50 days per annum – 25 officially organised by the FIA; the rest arranged as required by individual teams, who may use only 200 sets of tyres for testing.
- **A couple of changes have been made** following recent tribunal cases. There is now a section in the rule book about liveries (after BAR's failed attempt to run its cars in two different colour schemes). And the procedure for stop-go penalties has been clarified after the confusion surrounding Michael Schumacher at Silverstone last season.

Possible incidents

- **On the grid.**
  - **If something untoward happens before the start,** the official procedure is aborted and restarted from the five-minute board (here, the race distance will be reduced by one lap to compensate for the warm-up lap that has already taken place, because no further refuelling is permitted at this stage).
  - **If a car stalls once the start procedure is under way,** the car(s) affected will be indicated by flag marshals and will be allowed to start if they fire up without assistance or they may join in – belatedly – from the pits.
  - **If a driver jumps the start (detected by an electronic sensor),** he will be given a stop-and-go penalty and must pass through the pits at a prescribed time.
- **Race stoppages**
  - **If fewer than two laps have been completed,** the race will be started afresh and the distance will not be reduced. In this situation cars can be fettled and altered. If it is not possible to restart, no championship points will be awarded.
  - **If more than two laps but less than 75 per cent of the race have been completed,** the race result will be calculated as an aggregate of two parts and a restart will be ordered. Refuelling is permitted during the break, but you may not switch chassis. If a car is refuelled in the pits, it will take the restart from the back of the grid. The restart order will be determined by positions at the time that the race was halted. If it is not possible to continue the race, half-points will be awarded.
- **Rain**
  If there is a significant change in the weather between the warm-up and the race, a 15-minute acclimatisation session will be arranged. If it starts raining at the scheduled start time, the race director is authorised to delay the race by 10 minutes at a time. Rain does not provide a reason to stop a race unless conditions actually become dangerous.
- **Safety Car**
  If there is an incident that does not necessitate a race stoppage, the race director is empowered to order a Safety Car (SC) period. Drivers must line up behind the Safety Car and are not allowed to pass it. Each lap covered in this fashion counts towards the race distance and the contest restarts in anger when the Safety Car is withdrawn after the track has been cleared. Pit stops are permitted during these periods.

Statistics

F1 in figures

(Up to date to the eve of the 1999 Australian GP)

Grand Prix victories (drivers)

Alain Prost (FR)	51
Ayrton Senna (BR)	41
Michael Schumacher (GER)	33
Nigel Mansell (GB)	31
Jackie Stewart (GB)	27
Jim Clark (GB)	25
Niki Lauda (AU)	25
Juan-Manuel Fangio (ARG)	24
Nelson Piquet (BR)	23
Damon Hill (GB)	22
Stirling Moss (GB)	16
Jack Brabham (AUS)	14
Emerson Fittipaldi (BR)	14
Graham Hill (GB)	14
Alberto Ascari (IT)	13
Mario Andretti (USA)	12
Alan Jones (AUS)	12
Carlos Reutemann (ARG)	12
Jacques Villeneuve (CAN)	11
Gerhard Berger (AU)	10
James Hunt (GB)	10
Ronnie Peterson (SWE)	10
Jody Scheckter (RSA)	10
Mika Hakkinen (FIN)	9
Denis Hulme (NZ)	8
Jackie Ickx (BE)	8
René Arnoux (FR)	7
Tony Brooks (GB),	
Jacques Laffite (FR),	
Riccardo Patrese (IT),	
Jochen Rindt (AU),	
John Surtees (GB),	
Gilles Villeneuve (CAN)	6
Michele Alboreto (IT),	
Giuseppe "Nino" Farina (IT),	
Clay Regazzoni (SWI),	
Keke Rosberg (FIN),	
John Watson (GB)	5
David Coulthard (GB),	
Dan Gurney (USA),	
Bruce McLaren (NZ)	4
Thierry Boutsen (BE),	
Peter Collins (GB),	
Mike Hawthorn (GB),	
Phil Hill (USA),	

Didier Pironi (FR)	3
Elio de Angelis (IT),	
Patrick Depailler (FR),	
Froilan Gonzalez (ARG),	
Johnny Herbert (GB),	
Jean-Pierre Jabouille (FR),	
Peter Revson (USA),	
Pedro Rodriguez (MEX),	
Jo Siffert (SWI),	
Patrick Tambay (FR),	
Maurice Trintignant (FR),	
Wolfgang Von Trips (GER),	
Bill Vukovich (USA)	2
Jean Alesi (FR),	
Giancarlo Baghetti (IT),	
Lorenzo Bandini (IT),	
Jean-Pierre Beltoise (FR),	
Joachim Bonnier (SWI),	
Vittorio Brambilla (IT),	
Jimmy Bryan (USA),	
François Cevert (FR),	
Luigi Fagioli (IT),	
Pat Flaherty (USA),	
Heinz-Harald Frentzen (GER),	
Peter Gethin (GB),	
Richie Ginther (USA),	
Sam Hanks (USA),	
Innes Ireland (GB),	
Jochen Mass (GER),	
Luigi Musso (IT),	
Alessandro Nannini (IT),	
Gunnar Nilson (SWE),	
Carlos Pace (BR),	
Olivier Panis (FR),	
John Parsons (USA),	
Jim Rathmann (USA),	
Ludovico Scarfiotti (IT),	
Bob Sweikert (USA),	
Piero Taruffi (IT),	
Lee Wallard (USA),	
Rodger Ward (USA),	
Eddie Irvine (GB)	1

(Current drivers in bold)

World Champions (drivers)

- 1950. Giuseppe "Nino" Farina (IT. Alfa Romeo)
- 1951. Juan-Manuel Fangio (ARG. Alfa Romeo)
- 1952. Alberto Ascari (IT. Ferrari)
- 1953. Alberto Ascari (IT. Ferrari)
- 1954. Juan-Manuel Fangio (ARG. Maserati and Mercedes)
- 1955. Juan-Manuel Fangio (ARG. Mercedes)
- 1956. Juan-Manuel Fangio (ARG. Ferrari)
- 1957. Juan-Manuel Fangio (ARG. Maserati)
- 1958. Mike Hawthorn (GB. Ferrari)
- 1959. Jack Brabham (AUS. Cooper)
- 1960. Jack Brabham (AUS. Cooper)
- 1961. Phil Hill (USA. Ferrari)
- 1962. Graham Hill (GB. BRM)
- 1963. Jim Clark (GB. Lotus)
- 1964. John Surtees (GB. Ferrari)
- 1965. Jim Clark (GB. Lotus)
- 1966. Jack Brabham (AUS. Brabham)
- 1967. Denis Hulme (NZ. Brabham)
- 1968. Graham Hill (GB. Lotus)
- 1969. Jackie Stewart (GB. Matra)
- 1970. Jochen Rindt (AU. Lotus)
- 1971. Jackie Stewart (GB. Tyrrell)
- 1972. Emerson Fittipaldi (BR. Lotus)
- 1973. Jackie Stewart (GB. Tyrrell)
- 1974. Emerson Fittipaldi (BR. McLaren)
- 1975. Niki Lauda (AU. Ferrari)
- 1976. James Hunt (GB. McLaren)
- 1977. Niki Lauda (AU. Ferrari)
- 1978. Mario Andretti (USA. Lotus)
- 1979. Jody Scheckter (RSA. Ferrari)
- 1980. Alan Jones (AUS. Williams)
- 1981. Nelson Piquet (BR. Brabham)
- 1982. Keke Rosberg (FIN. Williams)
- 1983. Nelson Piquet (BR. Brabham)
- 1984. Niki Lauda (AU. McLaren)
- 1985. Alain Prost (FR. McLaren)
- 1986. Alain Prost (FR. McLaren)
- 1987. Nelson Piquet (BR. Williams)
- 1988. Ayrton Senna (BR. McLaren)
- 1989. Alain Prost (FR. McLaren)
- 1990. Ayrton Senna (BR. McLaren)
- 1991. Ayrton Senna (BR. McLaren)
- 1992. Nigel Mansell (GB. Williams)
- 1993. Alain Prost (FR. Williams)
- 1994. **Michael Schumacher (GER. Benetton)**
- 1995. **Michael Schumacher (GER. Benetton)**
- 1996. **Damon Hill (GB. Williams)**
- 1997. **Jacques Villeneuve (CAN. Williams)**
- 1998. **Mika Hakkinen (FIN. McLaren)**

(Current drivers in bold)

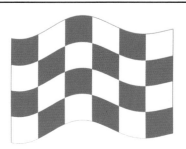

Grand Prix starts (drivers)

Riccardo Patrese (IT)	256
Gerhard Berger (AU)	210
Andrea de Cesaris (IT)	208
Nelson Piquet (BR)	204
Alain Prost (FR)	199
Michele Alboreto (IT)	194
Nigel Mansell (GB)	187
Graham Hill (GB) and Jacques Laffite (FR)	176
Niki Lauda (AU)	171
Thierry Boutsen (BE)	163
Ayrton Senna (BR)	161
Martin Brundle (GB)	158
John Watson (GB) and **Jean Alesi (FR)**	152
René Arnoux (FR)	149
Derek Warwick (GB)	147
Carlos Reutemann (ARG)	146
Emerson Fittipaldi (BR)	144
Jean-Pierre Jarier (FR)	135
Eddie Cheever (USA) and Clay Regazzoni (SWI)	132
Johnny Herbert (GB)	130
Mario Andretti (USA)	128
Jack Brabham (AUS)	126
Ronnie Peterson (SWE)	123
Pierluigi Martini (IT)	119
Michael Schumacher (GER)	118
Jackie Ickx (BE) and Alan Jones (AUS)	116
Keke Rosberg (FIN) and Patrick Tambay (FR)	114
Mika Hakkinen (FIN)	113
Denis Hulme (NZ) and Jody Scheckter (RSA)	112
John Surtees (GB)	111
Philippe Alliot (FR)	109
Elio de Angelis (IT)	108
Jochen Mass (GER)	105
Joachim Bonnier (SWI)	102
Bruce McLaren (NZ)	101
Damon Hill (GB)	100
Jackie Stewart (GB)	99
Rubens Barrichello (BR)	98
Chris Amon (NZ) and Jo Siffert (SWI)	96
Patrick Depailler (FR) and Ukyo Katayama (JAP)	95
Ivan Capelli (IT)	93
James Hunt (GB)	92
Jean-Pierre Beltoise (FR) and Dan Gurney	86
Jonathan Palmer (GB)	84
Marc Surer (SWI), Maurice Trintignant (FR), **Heinz-Harald Frentzen (GER)** and **Eddie Irvine (GB)**	82
Stefan Johansson (SWE)	79
Alessandro Nannini (IT)	77
Piercarlo Ghinzani (IT) and **Olivier Panis (FR)**	76
David Coulthard (GB)	75
Vittorio Brambilla (IT), Satoru Nakajima (JAP), Hans Stuck (GER) and Mauricio Gugelmin (BR)	74
Jim Clark (GB) and Carlos Pace (BR)	72
Stefano Modena (IT) and Didier Pironi (FR)	70
Bruno Giacomelli (IT)	69
Mika Salo (FIN)	68
Gianni Morbidelli (IT), **Pedro Diniz (BR)** and Gilles Villeneuve (CAN)	67
Stirling Moss (GB)	66
Teo Fabi (IT) and Aguri Suzuki (JAP)	64
J.J. Lehto (FIN)	62
Mark Blundell (GB)	61
Jochen Rindt (AU)	60
Erik Comas (FR)	59
Arturo Merzario (IT), Henri Pescaralo (FR) and Jos Verstappen (NL)	57
Alex Caffi (IT), Pedro Rodriguez (MEX) and Harry Schell (USA)	55
Rolf Stommelen (GER) and Philippe Streiff (FR)	54
Jean Behra (FR) and Richie Ginther (USA)	52
Juan-Manuel Fangio (ARG)	51
Mike Hailwood (GB), Innes Ireland (GB) and Jackie Oliver (GB)	50
Derek Daly (GB), Jean-Pierre Jabouille (FR), Nicola Larini (IT) and **Jacques Villeneuve (CAN)**	49
Phil Hill (USA)	48
Etc...	

(Current drivers in bold)

Pole positions (drivers)

Ayrton Senna (BR)	65
Jim Clark (GB)	33
Alain Prost (FR)	33
Nigel Mansell (GB)	32
Juan-Manuel Fangio (ARG)	28
Niki Lauda (AU)	24
Nelson Piquet (BR)	24
Damon Hill (GB)	20
Michael Schumacher (GER)	20
Mario Andretti (USA)	18
René Arnoux (FR)	18
Jackie Stewart (GB)	17
Stirling Moss (GB)	16
Alberto Ascari (IT)	14
James Hunt (GB)	14
Ronnie Peterson (SWE)	14
Jack Brabham (AUS)	13
Graham Hill (GB)	13
Jackie Ickx (BE)	13
Jacques Villeneuve (CAN)	13
Gerhard Berger (AU)	12
Mika Hakkinen (FIN)	11
Jochen Rindt (AU)	10
David Coulthard (GB)	8
Riccardo Patrese (IT)	8
John Surtees (GB)	8
Jacques Laffite (FR)	7
Emerson Fittipaldi (BR)	6
Phil Hill (USA)	6
Jean-Pierre Jabouille (FR)	6
Alan Jones (AUS)	6
Carlos Reutemann (ARG)	6
Chris Amon (NZ)	5
Nino Farina (IT)	5
Clay Regazzoni (SWI)	5
Patrick Tambay (FR)	5
Keke Rosberg (FIN)	5
Mike Hawthorn (GB)	4
Didier Pironi (FR)	4
Elio de Angelis (IT)	3
Tony Brooks (GB)	3
Teo Fabi (IT)	3
Froilan Gonzalez (ARG)	3
Dan Gurney (USA)	3
Jean-Pierre Jarier (FR)	3
Jody Scheckter (RSA)	3
Michele Alboreto (IT)	2
Jean Alesi (FR)	2
Stuart Lewis-Evans (GB)	2
Jo Siffert (SWI)	2
Gilles Villeneuve (CAN)	2
John Watson (GB)	2
Lorenzo Bandini (IT)	1
Rubens Barrichello (BR)	1
Joachim Bonnier (SWE)	1
Thierry Boutsen (BE)	1
Vittorio Brambilla (IT)	1
Eugenio Castellotti (IT)	1
Peter Collins (GB)	1
Andrea de Cesaris (IT)	1
Patrick Depailler (FR)	1
Giancarlo Fisichella (IT)	1
Heinz-Harald Frentzen (GER)	1
Bruno Giacomelli (IT)	1
Denis Hulme (NZ)	1
Carlos Pace (BR)	1
Mike Parkes (GB)	1
Tom Pryce (GB)	1
Peter Revson (USA)	1
and Wolfgang Von Trips (GER)	1

(Current drivers in bold)

Consecutive Grand Prix victories (drivers)

Alberto Ascari 9
(from the Belgian GP 52 to the Belgian GP 53)
Jack Brabham 5
(from the Netherlands GP to the Portuguese GP 60)
Jim Clark 5
(from the Belgian GP to the German GP 65)
Nigel Mansell 5
(from the South African GP to the San Marino GP 92)
Ayrton Senna 4
(from the British GP to the Belgian GP 88
and from the American GP to the Monaco GP 91)
Juan-Manuel Fangio 4
(from the Italian GP 53 to the French GP 54)
Jim Clark 4
(from the Belgian GP to the British GP 63)
Jack Brabham 4
(from the French GP to the German GP 66)
Jochen Rindt 4
(from the Netherlands GP to the German GP 70)
Alain Prost 4
(from the Canadian GP to the German GP 93)
Michael Schumacher 4
(from the Brazilian GP to the Monaco GP 94)
Damon Hill 4
(from the Australian GP 95 to the Argentinian GP 96)

(Current drivers in bold)

Grand Prix victories in a season (drivers)

Driver	Wins (Year)
Nigel Mansell	9 (1992)
Michael Schumacher	9 (1995)
Mika Hakkinen	8 (1998)
Damon Hill	8 (1996)
Ayrton Senna	8 (1988)
Michael Schumacher	8 (1994)
Jim Clark	7 (1963)
Alain Prost	7 (1984, 88 and 93)
Ayrton Senna	7 (1991)
Jacques Villeneuve	7 (1997)
Mario Andretti	6 (1978)
Alberto Ascari	6 (1952)
Jim Clark	6 (1965)
Juan Manuel Fangio	6 (1954)
Damon Hill	6 (1994)
James Hunt	6 (1976)
Nigel Mansell	6 (1987)
Ayrton Senna	6 (1989 and 90)
Michael Schumacher	6 (1998)

(Current drivers in bold)

Grand Prix victories (constructors)

Ferrari	120
McLaren	117
Williams	103
Lotus	79
Brabham	35
Benetton	27
Tyrrell	23
BRM	17
Cooper	16
Renault	15
Alfa Romeo	10
Ligier	9
Maserati	9
Matra	9
Mercedes	9
Vanwall	9
March	3
Wolf	3
Honda	2
Eagle, Hesketh, **Jordan**, Penske, Porsche and Shadow	1

(Current teams in bold)

World champions (constructors)

Year	Constructor	Year	Constructor
1958	Vanwall	1983	Ferrari
1959	Cooper-Climax	1984	McLaren-Tag-Porsche
1960	Cooper-Climax	1985	McLaren-Tag-Porsche
1961	Ferrari	1986	Williams-Honda
1962	BRM	1987	Williams-Honda
1963	Lotus-Climax	1988	McLaren-Honda
1964	Ferrari	1989	McLaren-Honda
1965	Lotus-Climax	1990	McLaren-Honda
1966	Brabham-Repco	1991	McLaren-Honda
1967	Brabham-Repco	1992	Williams-Renault
1968	Lotus-Ford	1993	Williams-Renault
1969	Matra-Ford	1994	Williams-Renault
1970	Lotus-Ford	1995	Benetton-Renault
1971	Tyrrell-Ford	1996	Williams-Renault
1972	Lotus-Ford	1997	Williams-Renault
1973	Lotus-Ford	1998	McLaren-Mercedes
1974	McLaren-Ford		
1975	Ferrari		
1976	Ferrari		
1977	Ferrari		
1978	Lotus-Ford		
1979	Ferrari		
1980	Williams-Ford		
1981	Williams-Ford		
1982	Ferrari		

Grand Prix victories in a season (constructors)

Constructor	Wins (Year)
McLaren	15 (1988)
McLaren	12 (1984)
Williams	12 (1996)
Benetton	11 (1995)
McLaren	10 (1989)
Williams	10 (1992 and 93)
McLaren	9 (1998)
Williams	9 (1986 and 87)
Benetton	8 (1994)
Lotus	8 (1978)
McLaren	8 (1991)
Williams	8 (1997)
Ferrari	7 (1952 and 53)
Lotus	7 (1963 and 73)
Tyrrell	7 (1971)
Williams	7 (1991 and 94)
Alfa Romeo	6 (1950 and 51)
Cooper	6 (1960)
Ferrari	6 (1975, 76, 79, 90 and 98)
Lotus	6 (1965 and 70)
Matra	6 (1969)
Etc...	

Grand Prix starts (constructors)

Constructor	Starts	Constructor	Starts
Ferrari	604	AGS	48
Lotus	490	Larrousse	48
McLaren	477	Wolf	48
Tyrrell	419	Gordini	40
Brabham	411	Honda	35
Williams	396	Theodore	34
Ligier	346	**Prost**	34
Arrows	322	**Stewart**	34
Benetton	268	Porsche	33
March	230	Penske	30
Minardi	222	Vanwall	28
BRM	198	Eagle	25
Lola	139	Forti	23
Osella	132	Pacific	22
Jordan	131	Simtec	21
Cooper	129	Rial	20
Renault	123	Lola-Haas	19
Surtees	117	Onyx	17
Alfa Romeo	112	Parnelli	16
Fittipaldi	104	Talbot	13
Shadow	104	Mercedes	12
ATS	99	Tecno	11
Ensign	99	Merzario	10
Sauber	98	Lancia	4
Dallara	78	**BAR**	1
Maserati	69		
Matra	61	*(Current teams in bold)*	
Zakspeed	54		
Hesketh	52		

Grand Prix victories (engines)

Engine	Wins	Engine	Wins
Ford	174	Maserati	11
Ferrari	120	BMW	9
Renault	95	Vanwall	9
Honda	71	Repco	8
Climax	40	Matra	3
Tag-Porsche	25	Mugen-Honda	2
Mercedes	21	Porsche	1
BRM	18	Weslake	1
Alfa Romeo	12		

The Girls

Jean-Marc Loubat
Vandystadt